Gabriella Braun is the Dire
consultancy firm using psy
to help leaders and teams.
clients including the British
and University of Cambridg
Consulting to Organisations:
Tavistock Clinic; and was a P
Consultancy Service.

'With her vast experience, hard-won insights and illuminating case studies, Gabriella Braun tells us what's really happening in that theatrical production we call work – and how we can give it a happier ending'

Michael Skapinker, *Financial Times* contributing editor and author of *Inside the Leaders' Club*

'A highly thoughtful, deeply sensitive and compelling account about the underlying motivations behind people's behaviour at work ... Beautifully written, it tells us what it means to be human at work'

Naomi Shragai, author of *The Man Who Mistook His Job For His Life*

'*All That We Are* takes as its starting point the fact that we, as humans, are messy and imperfect – especially when working together. This is not a book of easy answers and happy endings. It is about the difficult conversations and how to have them. These vignettes make a persuasive case for the catalysing effect of self-understanding'

Rónán Hession, author of *Leonard and Hungry Paul*

'Powerful, sensitive and timely. I wholeheartedly recommend this book'

Mike Brearley, former captain of England Cricket and President of the British Psychoanalytical Society

'This easily accessible book provides much insight about the behaviour of leaders and teams. And, captured by the stories, we are gently taken on a journey that will help us better understand our own inner theatre, thus making us more effective in our day-to-day life'

Manfred F. R. Kets de Vries, Distinguished Professor of Leadership, INSEAD

'So many books about organisational behaviour are dry or formulaic ... they are rarely a joy to read. Gabriella Braun digs deep to show us the unconscious patterns that shape our lives at work. The result is not just fascinating. It's gripping'

Christina Patterson, author of *Outside, the Sky is Blue*

'A sensitive and timely exploration into what is needed in order to create a more compassionate, positive and healthy workplace'

Fíona Scarlett, author of *Boys Don't Cry*

'For anyone committed to understanding and changing organisations this is a must read. This is a book I wish I had written'

Jennifer Petriglieri, author of *Couples That Work* and Associate Professor of Organisational Behaviour, INSEAD

'A stunning book and a must-read for anyone interested in psychology, our working lives, or simply what it means to be human'

Philippa East, author of *Little White Lies* and *Safe and Sound*

'This book is a delight. Refreshing and inspiring, healing even'

Gianpiero Petriglieri, Associate Professor of Organisational Behaviour, INSEAD

'An important book for all managers and leaders who care about their people and organisations'

Steven D'Souza, Senior Partner, Korn Ferry and author of *Not Knowing*

'A fascinating and insightful book that delves deep into how we can improve our time at work. But more than this, it shows us how we can create a more compassionate and kind society at large. A must read'

Neema Shah, author of *Kololo Hill*

'A timely and important book, it's a pleasure to read. The complex ideas are distilled into everyday language that readers can apply to their own workplace, deepening their understanding of what is going on below the surface. I warmly welcome and highly recommend this book'

Dr Jon Goldin, Consultant Child and Adolescent Psychiatrist, Great Ormond Street Hospital

ALL THAT WE ARE

Uncovering the Hidden Truths Behind Our Behaviour at Work

Gabriella Braun

PIATKUS

PIATKUS

First published in Great Britain in 2022 by Piatkus
This paperback edition published in 2023 by Piatkus

1 3 5 7 9 10 8 6 4 2

The organisations and people in this book are composites, anonymised and fictionalised in order to protect client confidentiality.

A CIP catalogue record for this book
is available from the British Library.

ISBN: 978-0-349-42730-0

Typeset in Sabon by M Rules
Printed and bound in Great Britain by Clays Ltd, Elcograf S.p.A.

Papers used by Piatkus are from well-managed forests
and other responsible sources.

FSC
www.fsc.org
MIX
Paper from
responsible sources
FSC® C104740

Piatkus
An imprint of
Little, Brown Book Group
Carmelite House
50 Victoria Embankment
London EC4Y 0DZ

An Hachette UK Company
www.hachette.co.uk

www.littlebrown.co.uk

In memory of my parents.

Contents

Part Three: Finding Ourselves

Introduction

Starting with Us

Remove the desks and chairs, the computers and cupboards, the factory floor or operating theatre and you have people. Just people. And everything we, as people, bring to our workplaces. Our hopes, our fears, our histories and personalities. Our thoughts and feelings, attitudes and beliefs, our understandable and unfathomable behaviours. We bring all that we are.

Work does far more than occupy our time and provide our livelihood. It provides an outlet for our intelligence and skills. It's part of our identity, a source of belonging and exclusion, of pleasure and pain. The dynamics of different relationships in the workplace, giving rise to issues of power, status, equality, camaraderie and competition, touch every one of us and every part of us. Much as we may want to, we cannot leave aspects of ourselves outside the building or virtual space when we go to work.

In that shared space, we create working norms and a common culture. They are influenced by wider society and the nature of the work – a hospital's ethos, for instance, differs from a car plant. The culture of each workplace is also affected by the personalities and psychological makeup of its leaders and staff. And, since organisations bring groups of people together, they are encrypted with the intricacies of what it means to be human.

Yet, we've spent years dehumanising the workplace in an attempt to exponentially increase productivity and profit. We've tried to rationalise and control our ways of working as if we were robots. In the process, we've created burnout cultures in which human beings fare badly. Our lives, and our mental health and well-being have suffered. So, ironically, has our work.

I help leaders and teams to be at their best by attending to the hidden, often unknown, motives behind their behaviour and the dynamics between them. I see the effect of stress and burnout on a daily basis. A team too demoralised, too stressed and anxious to even notice each other or say hello when they arrive in the office. A coaching client crying throughout the session, saying over and over, 'I've had enough. No more. I can't do it.' A team holding on by their fingernails under the relentless stress of treating highly disturbed and disturbing patients in an understaffed, under-resourced, mental health service.

The barrage of stress comes from all around: from the state of our politics and society; from clients, shareholders and stakeholders; from targets, the requirement for instant responses, the push to do more for less.

Stress also comes from within us. Our own push and pressure. Our own dismissal of the way our minds work.

In 2017 a UK government report, 'Thriving at Work: the Stephenson/Farmer Review of Mental Health and Employers', highlighted a growing and far greater mental health problem in the workplace than we had acknowledged. There followed a substantial increase in mental health first aid training.

But what does mental health first aid really change? It doesn't address the causes of mental ill health. At a time when funding of mental health treatment services has been drastically cut, it provides a sticking plaster. Of course, acknowledging the problem is important. As is reducing stigma, training staff to spot signs of mental health difficulties, to have conversations with colleagues and direct them to sources of help. It's a start, but it's insufficient.

We need to understand the issues behind the statistics. And the statistics are bad: work-related stress, depression and anxiety have continued to rise, with 602,000 cases reported in 2018/19, representing 44 per cent of all work-related illness and 12.8 million lost working days – 54 per cent of all working days lost because of ill health.

Bullying and harassment have also increased, revealing a demise in compassion and care. In 2019, France Télécom was found guilty of 'institutional harassment' after a spate of staff suicides, and the UK Post Office found guilty of wrongful prosecution of hundreds of branch managers. These extreme cases warn of the consequences when bullying spirals out of control and employees become dehumanised objects.

We can only change this by taking human nature and its implications in the workplace seriously. At the moment, it doesn't happen nearly often enough. We skim the surface of understanding, opting for easy tips and slick tools and formulas to solve our workplace problems and psychometric tests that reveal our personality type.

Our Myers–Briggs personality type profiles may enable a colleague and me to appreciate, rather than get irritated about, our different approaches to planning workshops. As a big picture person, I start with the overall aim of the workshop; as a details person, she starts with getting the right venue. But the Myers–Briggs Type Indicator (MBTI) cannot explain why my colleague is quick to feel excluded when we meet with clients, or why I'm quick to take responsibility that isn't mine. These traits are about the impact of our histories. Without this understanding, we'd remain stuck in patterns dictated by our unconscious response to those histories.

I think the reason we habitually discount the need for proper understanding of human nature in the workplace is fear. We fear the unknown and fear our lack of control. We choose ignorance as we prefer not to know that, ultimately, we cannot control whether our company gets taken over, our patients die or our students become criminals.

Having limited control over ourselves, let alone others, creates anxiety. We don't want to know how multifaceted we are. We don't want to know the chaos our minds can dissolve into. That as well as our aptitude for compassion, kindness and hope, we all have another side that breeds envy, violence and hatred. The knowledge of this frightens us.

So when things go wrong, we resolutely focus on visible, tangible activities: restructuring, introducing new processes or quality measures. Or mental health first aid training. We behave as if we don't have an unconscious and can neatly tuck our feelings and defences, insecurities and inadequacies under the pillow with our pyjamas, when we go to work. We cling to the illusion that organisations function like machines, and that mechanical solutions will save the day.

None of this prevents our true selves – the parts we know and the parts we don't – coming to work with us. It doesn't stop the different personalities, cultures, backgrounds and beliefs we find there, along with different pay grades, hierarchy and roles, creating a cauldron of emotions and reactions to situations and to each other. Many are out of our grasp in the unconscious, yet they affect us all the time. They are the reason, for instance, we react with equanimity one day, to the same thing that leaves us pulling our hair out the next; why we respond so heatedly to who sits where in the office; why, as leaders, we bend over backwards for one member of our team and come down like a ton of bricks on another. Or why our bosses can evoke such powerful and, at times, bewildering reactions from us.

There are some signs of change. We have woken up to the mental health crisis in the workplace and the damage caused by years of prioritising targets over professional judgements, speed over quality, simplistic solutions over complexity. We have begun to redress the culture with more compassionate attitudes and policies, such as flexible working that allows employees to fit their work and personal lives together.

In 2020, the Covid-19 pandemic plunged us into a depth of crisis most of us have never experienced. It turned our lives upside down. Suddenly, the fundamentals of our need as humans for close contact with others, to share physical space and touch, became potentially lethal. Our anxiety levels have rocketed. We are exhausted and traumatised. We have faced, and face, incomprehensible loss of life, of health, wealth, jobs and businesses. As we emerge and rebuild, the need to change our ways of working and living is more critical and urgent than ever.

If we can grasp it, recovery is an opportunity. But we have to go further than the shoots of change we saw before the pandemic when we considered our conscious mind but not the influence of the unconscious. We assumed a coherence in human beings that does not exist.

Rather than thinking solely about responding to mental ill health, we have the chance to finally support mental health and put it at the centre of how we work. To pay attention to all aspects of who we are and how we function: our creativity and passion, as well as our discontents and problems. But you cannot repair something broken or build something new without understanding the structure and materials you're using. And we cannot repair our dysfunctional ways of working or create environments in which people will thrive, without understanding human nature.

We need to strip away the outer layers and look at our inner workings. Psychoanalysis, which recognises the unconscious as well as the conscious mind, does just this. Applying it to organisational life brings a different lens – a magnifying glass – through which to see and understand people.

My experiences as an employee seeded this book. I had some great times and some utterly miserable times at work. I loved the camaraderie with colleagues, seeing students and staff develop when I worked in further education and in staff training and, working for a national awarding body, collaborating with people throughout the education and training sector to design new, progressive, qualifications. But when I became a leader, with no training and support, managed by the company bully, and struggling with my team of new staff, my stress escalated until I feared becoming ill.

I set up as a freelance consultant, designing national occupational standards and vocational qualifications in the UK, and was fortunate to work on education reform projects in Eastern Europe during the turbulent early 1990s. The work, particularly in different countries, was fascinating and I learnt a huge amount, but I wanted to go deeper into issues between people and within organisations, so I did a master's at the Tavistock Clinic in London: *Consultation and the Organisation: Psychoanalytic Approaches*. The course handbook strongly recommended having psychoanalysis or psychoanalytic psychotherapy. With this 'permission', I had an assessment with a psychoanalyst. I'd come, I said, because of the master's. He asked if it was the only reason. At that moment the pretence evaporated, and I allowed my previously unacknowledged need to look at my own issues come to the fore.

The master's and, in particular, my psychoanalysis, changed my thinking and my work. They put me on the path that led to this book. Having become frustrated by psychoanalytic thinking remaining largely unknown in organisations, and the inability of us consultants to take it out into the world, I set up a seminar series aimed at leaders with no psychological knowledge, from any industry. People could come to as many or as few seminars as they wanted. Each one explored a topic such as love, loss or persecution, and the relevance of psychoanalytic ideas to leadership. I illustrated the theory with stories, which we discussed in relation to participants' experience, whether they worked for the British Library, the Body Shop, Circus Space, a college or HM Revenue and Customs.

I soon realised the potential for a book; it's evolved a long way since the seminar series but the fact that people came along for two and a half hours after work, knowing nothing of psychoanalysis, and found the ideas relevant and fascinating, remained a strong motivation for me.

As the seminar participants soon learnt, taking psychoanalysis out of the therapy room and into the staffroom isn't about treating or analysing people. It's about applying the most sophisticated method we have for understanding human beings, to comprehend what happens to and between people at work. It's about connecting our internal worlds and individual histories with our behaviour and attitudes, and understanding the conditions that can trigger our destructiveness and those our constructive side needs to flourish in the workplace.

Organisations are systems though, not just individuals, so I also use ideas from open systems theory and systemic family therapy. These consider organisational design, structure, roles, authority, task and boundaries. They bring into focus threads we don't usually think about: how an organisation's past and aspirations for their future affects them in the present; the links, both conscious and unconscious, between the parts of an organisation that together form a whole system and between the organisation and the wider context it operates in.

I also use the notion of representation from systems theory: just as in a family a troubled child might unconsciously represent troubles within the whole family, at work different sections or individuals can represent issues for the whole system.

While theory informs my thinking, my work is about people, and this book is based on their stories. Stories help us make sense of our lives and experiences; they harness our imaginations and emotions. This helps us see behind the curtains and uncover the truth of our hidden selves in a unique way.

Part One of the book, *Human Nature at Work*, examines the fundamentals of our minds and their effect in the workplace. The following sections explore our essential contradiction. Part Two, *Losing Ourselves*, delves into the mire of our destructiveness and its ability to undo us in and out of work. Part Three, *Finding Ourselves,* highlights the inspiration and potential of our constructive side.

I hope in illuminating all that we are, and the significance of understanding ourselves and each other, this book will contribute towards workplaces becoming more creative, inclusive and humane communities in which people and their work flourish.

PART ONE

HUMAN NATURE AT WORK

1

The Choices We Don't Know We Make

I often questioned, and sometimes regretted, my decision to consult to the staff of a centre treating men addicted to drugs and alcohol. But I'd just got my master's degree and was keen to build up my consultancy practice. So, every fortnight, I spent almost four hours driving back and forth to Essex to run an hour-long session with the team. Whoever was on shift attended: the centre manager, counsellors, support workers, the administrator and the cook.

The residential centre occupied two former houses on a quiet, leafy street. There were twenty-five staff and places for fifteen clients. It's common for teams in such intense, highly demanding environments to have consultancy to enable them to make sense of and detoxify from its effects so they can work effectively. I'd had an initial meeting with the team to explore whether I could help them. They'd had a consultant before me, but she'd left some months before. They didn't say why.

We'd agreed to go ahead. The purpose of the sessions would be to support their work with clients by improving their teamwork.

Arriving early for the first session, I went to the overheated meeting room that, in the evenings, became the clients' lounge. Brian, the manager, arrived a few minutes later. Other staff straggled in and sat or sprawled on the tatty sofas and armchairs. One of the counsellors, Damian, had missed the exploratory session and introduced himself to me. TJ, the cook, came in last. He pulled up the only upright chair near the door.

I reminded them of the purpose of the sessions. Brian repeated what he'd said at our first meeting: their clients were hard work. The others sat mutely. I asked for examples. No response. A worrying client? An issue they struggled with? Nothing. People fidgeted in awkward silence until Damian protested: they didn't know what to do and I didn't tell them. Yes, the others agreed, why didn't I tell them what to do?

'The last staff group facilitator asked us each to speak in turn. Why don't you do that?' Damian asked. TJ instructed me to tell them all about myself. I should talk for about ten minutes.

'So you don't have to?' I asked. They ignored this.

Peter, a support worker, noticed I didn't have a wedding ring. Was I divorced? Single? Did I have children? Who did I live with?

I suggested they wanted to turn me into one of them, rather than use me as a consultant who might be able to help them improve the way they worked together.

'Bollocks.' Damian leaned forward, his voice raised. 'The whole organisation is fucking crap. Shite. Useless. No one knows what the hell they're doing. It's a fucking joke.'

Brian hit back. What did Damian ever do apart from moan and whinge? He'd messed up the rota last week when he suddenly went off ill, he hadn't informed Brian about a meeting yesterday. 'I'm the boss,' Brian said, 'but when do you ever do what I say?'

Their hostility electrified the room.

I went home tired and dispirited. I'd managed to get the team to talk, but failed to get them to think. We hadn't touched on what the fight between Brian and Damian meant or might represent for the whole team. We hadn't worked on our agreed purpose of reflecting on their teamwork in order to support their work with clients.

I recalled the preliminary meeting; why had I taken their agreement to work with me at face value? Clearly it had no meaning. I doubted it occurred to the team that they could say no to my becoming the next facilitator. What's a choice, if the people asked to choose don't believe they have one? But not choosing was itself a choice. And what about me? Had I made a clear choice to work with them? I wanted the work and, perhaps more importantly, I didn't want to get on the wrong side of the senior colleague who'd recommended me to the organisation. In a way, it was another non-choice.

Some of the team had worked at the centre for years, but others joined and left at an alarming rate. Sickness rates were shockingly high. The rota was a constant source of contention; it got changed all the time at short notice, so staff could never be sure of their hours. Some people always got the shifts they wanted; others never did.

Decisions were made and unmade and rules routinely broken. For instance, at the outset of their stay, clients committed to attending all their treatment sessions. When one of them kept missing these, Brian and the counsellors decided to issue him with a warning but then someone – I never found out who – unmade the decision and let the client off the hook.

In the third session, the team talked about their fury at losing the last facilitator. Brian had told her they didn't want to work with her anymore.

'An outright lie,' Damian said. Others agreed.

Brian insisted it wasn't, but it had taken two years from

deciding to let the facilitator go, to her actually leaving, and by then the people who had said they didn't want her anymore had also left.

'Crap,' Damian said.

I asked why it had taken that long but didn't get an answer. 'Perhaps you didn't want me to replace her.'

'That's not true,' Joy, the administrator, said.

'We didn't have a choice,' Damian jumped in.

'You did. But maybe you didn't believe that.'

They said they believed in fate. Things just happened; choice didn't come into it. I said that absolved them of their responsibility. That not choosing was a choice. That was how they'd chosen me.

'I loved her,' TJ said, taking the conversation back to the previous facilitator. 'I told her I did in her last session.'

He stared at me. Was he warning me that he'd always hate me because I'd taken her place? Or perhaps that he might direct his love towards me next? He already called me 'darling' when he saw me in the corridor before or after sessions.

My supervisor, who helped me think about my work, asked me how the sessions made me feel. I knew the importance of attending to my feelings; they provide rich data especially about unconscious communication from others.

'Anxious. A bit scared,' I admitted. 'I don't know if I'm up to this work.' I choked for a moment; what if taking on this project as a fledging consultant was a terrible mistake?

My supervisor pointed out that the staff might feel the same about working with the clients. Knowing that some of my doubts probably reflected the team's own doubts, reassured me a little.

I told my supervisor that I never knew where I was with the team, as though my feet couldn't find the ground, but that along with the stress – maybe because of it – I also got an adrenaline rush from the work. We thought about the way staff in organisations commonly soak up their clients' characteristics. Teachers sometimes become childish, theatres dramatic and addiction centres chaotic. Perhaps my experience linked to the centre's clients: the highs and lows, the need for the next fix dictating all.

Damian complained bitterly about everything, including me: I didn't understand anything; I was stupid and insensitive. The sessions were useless, even the purpose we'd agreed for them was wrong. 'It's about the clients. What about us?'

'Yes,' Eric, a support worker, agreed. 'Everything's always about the clients. We never get anything. Or not anything we want. We keep asking for wild mushroom risotto and get bloody cornflakes.'

'I guess I'm the cornflakes,' I said.

'And,' someone else said, as if I hadn't spoken, 'you have to buy the goddamn cornflakes yourself.'

I thought of the resentment and rage that caring for others can provoke, especially when you feel uncared for yourself. I ventured a comment about this but, as usual, got nowhere. I didn't know what to do.

Brian was manager in name only. He didn't manage the team or the centre. He did nothing about the chaos and absence of rules that left both staff and clients unsafe. In the power vacuum Brian left, Damian became the unnamed, unofficial leader and led the team in a war against the organisation. He accused Brian of not organising anything, mixing up the shifts, letting some staff get away with anything and everything.

Brian and Damian's fights took centre stage during most sessions, but periodically other fights erupted. Sometimes TJ provoked the others, swearing and yelling for no apparent reason. People rarely said anything, seeming to cower in response. Once Brian accused a counsellor of needing too much reassurance. It turned out she was leaving the next day. I didn't understand Brian's reasons for lashing out at her on her last day. I asked the team whether perhaps they handled the pain of endings by fighting, but my question got no traction.

I spent most of the first six months struggling to understand what was going on. So much was withheld from me and expressed indirectly through a confusing smokescreen of emotion and behaviour. It reminded me of the early days as a patient in psychoanalysis when I spent many sessions in the grip of my unconscious reactions. The night before my first session I'd dreamt I could barely reach the steering wheel and couldn't see out of the windscreen of the car I was driving. My unconscious was right; I couldn't see the way or steer anything in analysis. Memories and feelings appeared unbidden. I understood little and could control less, as I went from moment to moment in a tumult of emotions.

I suspected the team were in a similar state; governed by their unconscious, unable to make sense of it or have agency over themselves. With the safety of the analytic process and expertise of my analyst, I'd moved out of this initial phase to a place of gathering insights where I felt less thrown around by my own storms. But this hadn't happened to the team so far and I doubted my ability to help them get there.

Damian's vitriol against the place continued. I felt helpless in its wake. The team became increasingly immobilised, too, watching on impassively. Eventually I realised Damian was stuck in a horribly destructive relationship with the organisation. He enjoyed his cruelty and rage, yet also suffered from the poison of his contempt. My understanding gave me a way in.

'It must be painful to see the organisation as so useless, so crap and yet still be here,' I said. Damian stopped mid-rant.

The next session, the same thing happened; Damian ranted with explosive fury. I focused again on his inability to go: 'It must be so painful to think the organisation is so bad but not be able to leave.'

From then on, whenever he mounted a verbal assault on the centre, I repeated myself. After three months, Damian resigned.

My supervisor told me I'd done well. Damian needed to leave for the sake of the clients, the staff and, not least, for himself. His contemptuous, perverse relationship to the place was damaging for him and everyone around him.

The atmosphere improved after he left. I wondered if TJ would take over the fight but from the outset he'd mostly slept in the sessions. For months I tried to address this by encouraging him to say what was going on for him or questioning and interpreting why he slept. I'd given up. The truth was TJ frightened me. I preferred him asleep.

The rest of the team began to work with me, tentatively offering information about the impact of being employed at the centre. A year after I started working with them, they finally began to trust me. 'Because you've survived,' my supervisor said. 'It's been crucial for them. Other people come and go but you stay. You don't retaliate like Brian does and you bounce back from whatever they throw at you.'

One day I arrived to see police leaving the centre. Clients had been caught stealing from local shops. I started to ask about this, but Brian interrupted me.

'I'm more worried about them going out at night to do God knows what.'

'What?' Joy asked.

Others shuffled in their seats, looking away. Many of them had kept quiet and covered up for the night workers who were meant to stop clients going out because of the risk of them drinking or taking drugs. I asked about the night workers' collusion. Brian shrugged, the support workers giggled, TJ snored. I said nothing, feeling defeated.

After a few minutes I galvanised myself. 'Talk to me.'

Perhaps they picked up the defeat and desperation in my voice – the counsellors started to talk about their clients' childhoods. Some had been in care; many didn't know their fathers; the parent or main carer of others had died when they were children.

'I imagine in that context, depending on a substance is easier than depending on a person,' I said.

'You bet,' Brian agreed.

I suggested that since our parents or carers are our first authority figures, the clients' negative role models explained their dislike and suspicion of authority. Instead of protecting them, and giving them the security of solid boundaries, consistency and reliability, in the clients' experience, authority figures let them down and left them unsafe.

Brian said that the team understood the clients because many of them also had histories of addiction. In fact, some of them had been treated at the centre. They'd left and worked elsewhere before returning as staff – that was the rule. But they shared the clients' issues.

Suddenly, I understood: the staff had swapped their addiction to substances for an addiction to the centre. That was why Damian struggled to leave. That was why many of the staff, like the clients, hated authority. I was seeing first-hand the three different purposes that operate in organisations. The official purpose, the purpose staff believe they're carrying out and the unconscious purpose in the mind which staff are unaware of.

The centre's official purpose was to treat addicts. That's what they were funded for and what staff were paid for. The staff believed they were helping their clients to improve their lives. But both of these were almost incidental. Day by day, hour by hour, the team were governed by the unconscious purpose of using the centre and their jobs as an alternative addiction. It distorted their work and their thinking. It minimised the gap between clients and staff, making them almost indistinguishable from one another.

We all use our jobs and organisations to work out our internal issues, so this wasn't surprising. But it was an extreme example of the powerful effect of the unconscious in the workplace. The team demonstrated the way the unconscious influences our choice of profession and organisation. How it colours the dynamics and relationships between people and the way we respond to authority. The way the unconscious shapes an organisation's purpose and the delivery of its work. I saw how much the unconscious influences choices we don't know we make. In this organisation it ruled; the team repeatedly acted out the dictates of their unconscious and made choices unknowingly.

I knew I had to help them become aware of their unconscious purpose and its effect on their work. Ultimately, the staff needed to realign to the centre's purpose or, if they couldn't, like Damian, they needed to leave.

I hurried in from the rain on a cold February afternoon, nine months after Damian had left. The centre had been inspected and given a damning report. Brian was off ill and the staff didn't know what was wrong or when he'd be back.

'What good am I doing?' I asked my supervisor in desperation. 'I don't know half of what's going on. The inspection pointed to a big problem with clients' medication – giving it on time, monitoring, adjusting amounts – and they've never even mentioned it. It's like working blindfolded, with my hands tied behind my back.'

'You don't know a lot of what's going on because they don't tell you. But they're telling you more and more as time goes by and they learn to trust you.'

'What about realigning to the organisation's purpose? I've got nowhere with that. I don't know why I'm there.'

My supervisor fixed his eyes on mine. 'You're expecting too much, too fast. They can't suddenly realign. You're undoing the unconscious purpose they've had for a long time and are very invested in. And now Brian's off, you can't expect them to do more than keep going.'

I calmed down briefly, before anxiety gripped me again. 'But what if there are really dodgy things going on, worse than we know about and by staying there I'm colluding?'

We agreed to come back to this, but for now to take my worry as important information that might reflect the team's fears as well as my own.

Brian never returned. After three months of sick leave, he left; no reason was ever given. Abandoned once more by unreliable authority figures, the staff's rage resumed. Unconsciously, they identified me with management and everything it stood for: useless, careless, non-existent or even abusive authority that exploited staff's addiction to the organisation to get away with such poor leadership. For a while they verbally attacked me with even more voracity than before. We had to rebuild our relationship and trust all over again.

The session at the end of July started normally; TJ fell asleep, then grunted in cross surprise when Joy nudged him awake. He looked through half-closed eyes around the room.

'Leave me alone. You all shut up.'

Peter laughed and poked him again. 'Come on, wake up. We have these sessions in the afternoon so you're finished in the kitchen but you just sleep.'

Peter valued the sessions now and had found the courage to stand up for them. Eric and a couple of others backed him saying to TJ this was helpful, and he should join in.

TJ growled. 'Anyway' – he turned on Eric – 'who're you to

talk? Not even a proper man.' Silence. Eric's head bent almost to his knees, for a moment I mistook the strange sounds he emitted for laughter. He was crying.

'That's cruel, TJ,' I said, instantly regretting identifying TJ as the cruel one, instead of commenting on cruelty in the organisation. I asked them what was going on.

They told me a client had gone into the kitchen that morning and got hold of a large knife. He'd brandished it at Eric, who'd run out.

'That must have been really frightening,' I said to Eric. His nod was almost imperceptible.

'It's not fair to say he's not a proper man,' Joy said to TJ.

'A man doesn't run. A man fights,' TJ said.

'No, TJ,' I said. 'Out on the streets all that does is increase violence and add to the number of stabbings and deaths. And in here you're in positions of authority and responsibility. You absolutely cannot fight.'

I knew that in issuing instructions, I'd turned into the manager, something consultants should avoid, but at this moment it seemed vital.

I told the team that in the absence of a manager, we had to report this incident to the trustees. Once they knew, the trustees brought in an experienced locum, who quickly established his authority and had a calming influence on the centre. After two months, he got the job as the permanent manager. He combined firmness and clarity with support and care. As the gap between the staff and the clients grew, staff became more stable and competent and the centre was safer. With an effective manager in place, I also became more competent. I addressed the team's unconscious purpose and, as we brought it into consciousness, the addictive purpose that had dominated began to subside. Staff adhered to the official purpose, with its potential to help the clients' quality of life.

Six months after the new manager started, I bumped into Damian at London Bridge Station. He told me leaving the centre had been the best thing he'd done in a long time. Everything about him seemed lighter. His unconscious addiction to the organisation had seeped like toxins into the walls, the furniture and into the other staff. Yet Damian had let me help him bring his unconscious choice into consciousness, found his agency and consciously chosen to sever the rotten umbilical cord.

He'd stayed in touch with a couple of the team and knew that other staff had also moved on.

'They're doing well. Staying off the drugs, still sober and happier in their work. I see Brian from time to time you know. Now that we're not working together, we get on. He's in a much better place and I know the team and the centre are too.'

'That's great,' I said. I wondered if Brian's departure also marked the movement from an unconscious to a conscious choice.

'What about you?' he asked. 'I heard you've decided to leave.'

I confirmed that I was going at the end of the month.

I'd decided the team were in a good enough place for me to move on. After working with them for more than two and a half years, I was both sad and glad to go. It had been gruelling at times, but I'd grown fond of the team and had learnt so much. I'd understood that effective consultancy doesn't necessarily look impressive; simply keeping going can be a measure of success. Neither does consultancy have to result in large change; sometimes the smallest step forward is huge. And I'd begun forging my identity and style as a consultant, working in a way which was true to psychoanalytic and systems thinking, but also true to me.

2

Safety and Security

'You won't remember me,' Rachel said. 'I came to your paper about attachment and the workplace.' She had rung to ask me for coaching. The new chief executive of the company she worked for had announced a major restructure. Morale plummeted as large numbers of staff faced redundancy. Some of the best people had already left. Two of Rachel's team had resigned; the others were looking for jobs. Sickness rates soared and performance crashed.

As soon as I saw her, I recalled Rachel sitting in the front row at my presentation, looking slightly aloof. I showed her into my consulting room. She sat on the sofa, her red hair a striking contrast against her brown trouser suit.

I asked her to tell me her story: her childhood, schooling, career and her family. Born in the north of England, Rachel's father had served in the army and the family lived in army bases, moving every two to three years. She went to boarding school at the age of eleven, went to university, got a job in London. She wasn't married.

No one had told me their story so fast or so minimally. I asked about siblings. One sister. Her parents? Still alive and together. They lived in Hertfordshire. I tried asking about each parent independently. Her mother's parents lived in Yorkshire; Rachel rarely saw them. Dad's parents, in their forties when he was born, died when Rachel was a child.

'What was boarding school like?' I enquired, trying to connect with this young woman.

She'd had a few friends, but never joined the 'in-group', an exclusive clique of the most popular girls. I imagined her, young and vulnerable, sent away from her family and then excluded at school.

Rachel bent down to pick up her bag. Putting it on the sofa beside her, she peered in it, rummaged around but retrieved nothing. Scrunching up her eyes, her face showed emotion for the first time.

'I learnt to hide my homesickness and loneliness,' she said. 'I was very unhappy.' She'd constantly worried about her mum. 'Her depression got worse when I went to boarding school. She always wanted a career, but we moved too much. Anyway, Dad put a stop to it. He thought women should look after the home and the children.'

Rachel rubbed the bridge of her nose. 'Mum lived on antidepressants.'

Listening to her struggles at university, her unhappiness in jobs and her frequent career and house moves, I realised Rachel had always felt unwanted and insecure.

'I said I wasn't married, but I have been. Twice. And divorced. I can't do long-term relationships. No children. My sister's got two bright and beautiful children. A good marriage.' Her mouth twisted with bitterness. 'She's the prodigal son, except she's a girl. The apple of our parents' eyes. She excelled at school and at sports. She's much prettier than me, had more friends, more boyfriends. Numerous boyfriends. Husband's a barrister. Earns a bomb.'

The buzz of her phone interrupted us. 'I thought I'd turned

it off,' she muttered, distracted. 'Do you mind?' Her thumbs sped over the keys.

'I would've loved children,' she went on, putting her phone aside. 'It's too late now.' Her eyes sought mine momentarily before darting away. 'Early menopause.'

We sat quietly. She picked up her phone again, glanced at the screen and put it back down beside her. 'I ring my parents every day you know. I often go on holiday with them.' I wasn't sure how to understand this or why she'd said it.

'You probably think that's sad,' she added. 'It's not as though we're close really. So why do I spend so much time with them?'

I didn't say anything.

'I suppose I'm still trying to win their approval and love.' She looked away.

'That must be painful,' I said. Rachel nodded.

I glanced at the clock: halfway through the one and a half hour session. I needed to return to her difficulties in her job. I asked if she saw any connections between her story and her situation at work.

'Apart from my insecure attachment pattern?' she laughed, referring to my paper and John Bowlby's attachment theory. I suspected she was right, that she'd always been insecure about her parents' care and reliability, and it had shaped the way she related to people.

Our pattern of attaching to key people in our lives – whether securely or insecurely – is set in childhood and continues throughout life. Children with a secure attachment to their parents (or carers) grow up with a benign trust in their place in their family and in the world. They have the security of knowing they can rely on their parents to love and care for them. The external trust and security are replicated in their internal world where they have trusted figures to turn to at times of need.

Like all those with insecure attachments, Rachel didn't have this psychological safety. She found the upheaval of change at work particularly difficult. Without an attachment to her job, the organisation or to her colleagues, she felt unmoored and unsafe.

Her relationship with her boss, Zach, the new chief executive, had made things worse. He frowned on Rachel working from home, yet often let her colleague, Tania.

Rachel claimed Tania got all the best clients. 'All the most interesting work goes to the people Zach likes best. And if you annoy him, even by disagreeing about something small, he punishes you, usually by not giving you new clients for a while, which affects your targets.'

Only direct client work counted against the targets, so those like Rachel who generated clients for the team, repeatedly failed to meet them.

'Every month Zach names and shames us about our targets at the team meeting. It's hideous. I can't stand it. I don't sleep the night before and feel sick afterwards.'

Rachel worried about her team. What if performance went downhill even further and more people left? She described each of them. The one she liked best, because he was reliable and hard-working. 'He flirts a little with me. That's why I like him best really.' The man she didn't like because he badgered her until she let him work on the most interesting projects. The 'needy' man Rachel avoided because he wanted constant advice and far more one-to-one meetings than anyone else. A woman who criticised everything: a meeting was too long or too short or too rushed; a client charged too much or too little.

I suggested these minor complaints might be a reaction to Rachel's authority and her role as the boss, not about her as a person. Rachel couldn't see the difference between them. The woman had even criticised her taste; how was that not personal? 'I admired someone's dress and she said it was risqué.'

'That sounds like a difference of opinion rather than a criticism,' I said.

She ignored this, telling me about another woman she avoided, especially on Mondays and Fridays. 'I can't bear hearing about her weekends. Her life's so lonely and sad. I don't know what to do about it.'

'Why is it your job to do anything?' I asked.

'I'm her boss, I have to.'

'You're the boss at work, not in your team's private lives.'

'I thought you advocated caring for people,' Rachel retorted. 'Surely you're not saying to wipe my hands of my team when they leave the office? That would be totally uncaring.' She smiled triumphantly.

I saw that although Rachel took even the mildest criticism injuriously and imagined it when it didn't exist, she had no trouble criticising others. I wondered what had brought out the viper in her now. Had I pushed a button to do with being the over-responsible child? Her guilt about not taking her mother's depression away and abandoning her by being at boarding school, going off to university and then to London?

I asked whether she might feel over-responsible towards her staff as perhaps she had towards her mother. Rachel acknowledged that she still felt responsible for her mother. 'So, you mean I can care about my team without taking the responsibility too far?' she said, in a mix of relief and disbelief.

'Exactly,' I replied. I went on to suggest that the way she related to each of her team depended on how they made her feel. She looked bemused.

'Maybe you're looking at their behaviour from your point of view rather than theirs,' I explained. 'You can't stand clinging for example, so you see someone who wants emotional closeness or physical proximity as needy.'

'You've got a point ... How ridiculous is that? I suppose it's my insecurity. Avoiding people, I mean, if they make me feel bad.'

'It seems like that.'

'Shit. I can't believe I'm doing that.' She paused. 'I think my favouritism pits the team against each other. Like Zach.' She looked out of the window, adding quietly, 'And like my parents.'

Twisting a lock of her hair around her forefinger, Rachel speculated that her problem with any hint of favouritism at work was because of her parents' favouritism towards her sister.

'I don't think I felt too loved by my parents. It made me insecure. I feel insecure most of the time if I'm honest. And I struggle to trust people.'

Rachel arrived late for her second session. She began by telling me she'd wished her parents had taken more interest in her. She couldn't remember them telling her off or praising her. They wanted her to do well at school but didn't want to know the details. There was no discussion about what subjects she'd take; she chose her A levels because the subjects seemed relatively easy. Assuming she wasn't intelligent enough to do a science degree, she'd settled for sociology.

At the age of fifteen, Rachel worried about her slightly inverted left nipple. She went to the family doctor during the school holidays. He asked if she'd talked to her mother. It hadn't even occurred to her to tell her mum she'd made an appointment with him.

I didn't see Rachel for another two months because of her crazy work schedule. When we finally met, she was late again. She'd gone from slim to thin. Her hair looked dull and her outfit thrown together without her usual care. She flung herself and her bag onto the sofa.

'I can't take it anymore. I don't trust Zach. He promises me new opportunities, but they never materialise. Instead, my boring, meaningless work multiplies all the time. I'm exhausted.' Her eyes welled up. 'Sorry. I don't know what's wrong with me.'

'You're upset.'

'Yes, I am. I've tried talking to Zach. He doesn't listen. I mean he says he is, but he isn't. I'm not developing an iota. Zach promises me it'll change but it doesn't.'

We talked about her rage at Zach's preferential treatment of Tania, her workplace sister, and how the unfairness provoked the same painful feelings as her actual sister did.

Tears trickled down her cheeks. She looked around the room as she wiped them away.

'I like that.' She pointed at the picture above the fireplace. 'I like the colours. It's playful.' She sighed. 'I can't remember the last time I felt playful at work.'

'You need to feel reasonably safe and secure to play,' I said.

She blew her nose, dabbed her eyes and got her phone out. She reminded me of a child holding their teddy bear or blanket.

Rachel went on to talk about the clique at work that went out for drinks and had lunch together. Some of them met up to go to the cinema or theatre. She'd never been invited. 'It's fine. I don't like mixing friendship and work.'

'I imagine the exclusion hurts though,' I said.

'Yes.'

'Like at boarding school.'

'What? Oh. Yes, it's like bloody boarding school.' She looked down at the phone in her lap.

How do you manage your needs, I thought, when you've

been sent away and your mother needs you more than you're allowed to need her?

Rachel was late again for the next session. I asked if it connected with the insecure attachment pattern she'd mentioned in our first session.

'I don't know,' she said. 'I didn't think of that. I'm always late. Especially for things that matter to me.'

'This matters to you then.'

'Yes, it seems to. Actually, that makes me a bit anxious.'

'In case I let you down?'

She nodded.

After that, Rachel started arriving on time for her sessions. She'd greet me with a smile, saying, 'On time again,' as I opened the door. Over the next few sessions, she turned her focus from what she couldn't do at work, to what she could do. She couldn't join the in-group, but she could do something about her leadership. She worked hard at this: she stopped avoiding some of her team, didn't give in to the badgering man and spent less time with the flirtatious one.

She started to think about each of her team members' individual needs. Listening properly to the man she'd judged as 'needy', she now heard the anxiety behind some of his questions. She told me the sad and lonely woman had joined a choir. Now that Rachel had let go of feeling responsible for everything, she found herself beginning to enjoy getting to know her team.

Rachel didn't instantly turn into a great manager of people, but she did reduce her team's anxiety and expand their psychological safety and security. She decided to end coaching. I suggested, as gently as I could, that perhaps her fear of attachment meant she was prematurely detaching, but she couldn't hear me.

Months later, Rachel emailed me. She'd resigned. She'd

never broken into the inner circle. She still felt lonely, an outsider. Tania and Zach still enraged her.

I thought of Rachel's first words to me. 'You won't remember me,' she'd said, based on her assumption that, unlike her sister, she'd always be invisible and forgotten. Without the safety and security of a solid attachment to people in her mind or her life, Rachel did what she always did when she felt hurt and needy. She uprooted herself, moved on and started again.

3

Life and Death

Appelby House stood at the end of a long gravel driveway with sweeping lawns on either side. I imagined Jane Austen's Emma looking down from a perfectly proportioned window or strolling out of the dusky blue door and plucking a white rose rambling up the side of the entrance porch.

Pauline, consultant psychiatrist and director, met me by the front door of the private residential service for children with eating disorders. Her face pale without makeup, her hair pulled back roughly, she told me a girl had jumped from her bedroom window while home for the weekend.

'She's OK, but apparently if she'd landed two centimetres to the left, a jagged iron bar would have killed her.' Pauline's voice shook. My breath caught as I tried to take this in.

We walked up the wide, curving staircase to a meeting room. 'She's thirteen,' Pauline continued, as she steadied herself against the banister. 'She was doing so well. Or so I thought. Making friends here, even starting to think about a family holiday in the summer. I really thought she'd be ready for that.'

The other two senior leaders – Marcus, head of administration and finance, and Sinead, head of nursing – were already in the room when we entered.

'You know?' Sinead asked. I nodded.

Staff drifted in talking quietly among themselves: the dietician, family therapists, teachers, nurses, psychiatrists, psychotherapists and psychologists, as well as the administrative and residential staff. I knew they'd face a punitive enquiry: why had they let the girl go home for the weekend? Pauline would be held accountable.

Helen, a psychotherapist, spoke quietly, 'I didn't see this coming.'

'If anyone's to blame it's me,' Pauline said. 'I'm her psychiatrist. But no matter what we do, we can't know who will attempt suicide. None of us foresaw this.'

Helen blinked back tears.

I'd worked with this team for a year, helping them to communicate across the different disciplines and digest and manage their dynamics so they could be at their best. I'd heard their fear – terror – for the children's lives many times. Eating disorders have the highest death rate of all psychiatric illnesses, and suicide attempts and severe self-harm are common. I knew there were always some children on round-the-clock observation, but this was the first attempted suicide in my time with the team. Now, I appreciated emotionally, as well as intellectually, the reality they lived with every day.

Their voices expressed concern as they talked about the staff closest to the girl. But when the therapists questioned the nurses about the events leading up to the weekend, the atmosphere changed.

'You don't know what it's like working such long hours with the patients,' Neil, a senior nurse, said, his foot tapping the floor. 'It's different for you therapists. You just see them for an hour. You don't have to get them to eat, clean the wounds when they deliberately cut themselves, reassure desperate parents. It's not you who has to restrain a child to get a glucose shot into them to keep them alive.'

'Here we go,' Helen sighed. 'There's nothing that upsets me more than this notion that you nurses do all the work and the rest of us don't pull our weight.'

'That's not what I'm saying.' Neil looked exasperated. His foot tapped faster.

'You don't appreciate our work,' Helen retorted. 'We have back-to-back appointments. We work long hours with the patients too, with their self-harm and suicidality. We also deal with highly anxious parents and manage risk.'

'I give up,' Neil groaned, looking up at the ceiling.

'Let's not do this,' Pauline said.

A dull pain throbbed above my left eyebrow. Why hadn't I seen this before? The repeated refrain that one discipline took the load and the others didn't appreciate them, sprung from their anxiety about death. I told them they always faced the tension between life and death and when death took centre stage, as it had now – and often did – anxiety overwhelmed them. That was when, I suggested, this friction between them reared up. A few people nodded.

One of the family therapists talked about the bitter custody battle between the girl's parents. 'Dad fights us, too. He constantly complains that we don't reply fast enough or thoroughly enough to his emails, we don't meet him often enough—'

'Oh please, we give him more time than any other parent,' Sinead interrupted.

'That's what I'm saying. He makes out that we don't do right by his daughter when actually we fall over backwards for her.'

'He's a bully,' Sinead said. 'He doesn't just document every meeting, every communication, but tells us he's doing that. He deliberately intimidates us.'

As they talked about her father, the girl herself got lost, as if her dad was their patient.

'Sometimes I hate him. That's awful, isn't it?' Helen said.

'He seems to invite your hatred,' I said.

The family therapist leaned forward, opened his mouth but closed it again. He waited for someone else to finish talking. 'I don't know if we should have taken her, given the custody battle.'

A hush fell across the room. I waited. Helen commented that the children who did best were the ones whose parents pulled together to help them.

'Maybe attempting suicide is the only way this girl can get her parents' attention,' I said.

'But it's so destructive, so self-hating,' Neil said.

'Hateful to us and to her parents. She's punishing us all. Not knowingly, but she is,' Helen added.

'I know I shouldn't be, but I'm bloody angry with her,' Neil said. 'Her key worker's really cut up. Maybe just as well it's his day off, although if he was in, we could at least support him.'

Smells of roasting chicken from the kitchen below reminded me of the time. As my stomach rumbled, I realised it had unclenched now the team had climbed out of the pit of friction and blame through voicing and making sense of their difficult feelings. To remind them of the link between their work and their dynamics, something we'd often explored, I asked about the impact of the children on them.

'They aren't like other patients; the children hate us because we try to make them better,' Pauline said, 'and that's the last thing they want.'

'They regularly reject and punish you for helping them,' I replied. 'It must make you occasionally hate them too.'

I thought of our opposing drives. The side of us that strives not just to stay alive, but to live our lives, versus the side of us pulling away from life, towards death. And with them, our extraordinary capacity for love, compassion and empathy, for hope and kindness. Our equally powerful capacity for hate and indifference, cynicism and cruelty; the insidious nullification and giving up on life of our death drive. Those days we want to hide under the blanket and retreat, not bother to look after ourselves, fight for a better world or have a difficult conversation.

Most of the time, the struggle between these two parts of us is hidden in our unconscious, but in this team, where the children's death drive dominated, and life and death tussled continuously, the pull between them was tangible. The threat of death loomed like a battle tank waiting just beyond the green space where children played.

I commented on the exertion needed to stay with life and resist the children's powerful pull towards death.

'The children drive me nuts sometimes, but I find the parents way harder,' a young nurse said. 'Some are great, but others . . .'

'I know,' a family therapist agreed. 'But for parents, Appelby is the end of the road. They hand over their children – their babies – having tried everywhere and everything else. They're desperate. That's why they put so much pressure on us.'

'Like asking us why their child isn't improving, why they've eaten fewer calories today than yesterday,' the young nurse added.

'I forget their anxiety sometimes. It's such a complex, awful illness. It's horrendous for the parents. This conversation reminds me of that, and makes me more sympathetic to the girl's father,' Helen said.

The team decided to refer the girl's parents for therapy.

They also thought about how to increase support for the nurses who received so much of the raw anxiety from both the parents and children.

'Just knock on my door,' the family therapist said. 'You can always offload to me and we can think about what's going on for the families.'

As I drove back up the driveway, I thought about the team's resilience. In one hour-long session, they'd rediscovered their compassion for the girl and her mum and dad, as well as for the other parents. And, in finding their compassion for one another again, they'd returned to collaborating and supporting each other.

A few months later, the company that owned Appelby sold the beautiful premises. In the first session at the new place, I found staff downcast and angry. The contrast between the old building and this one hit me as soon as I entered. The place was shabby, cramped and dark. An acrid smell hung in the air. The team sat jammed together, listless and sullen as Pauline tried to boost their morale, telling them they were over the worst now. She asked for volunteers to run extra sessions with parents who, worried about the effect on their children, were furious about the move, and even more anxious than usual. No one responded. The slow spread of despondency had claimed them. I, too, struggled not to give up. Only Pauline, Marcus and Sinead retained their commitment and passion for Appelby's existence and work.

Setting off for our session the next month, I felt apprehensive, but the team had spruced the place up with plants, rugs and pictures. Even the smell had gone. I'd underestimated their drive for life.

One Friday at 6p.m., six months after they'd moved, Pauline rang me. Appelby was being closed because it cost too much. I gulped down the bile in my mouth. How could this happen to such a crucial and excellent service? Why did money and profit come before care?

A few days later, Pauline, Marcus, Sinead and I gathered in a small, badly lit room. The stale air clung to scratched furniture and a threadbare carpet.

'I should have realised they wanted to close us down,' Pauline said.

'How could you have known?' Marcus asked.

'None of us did,' Sinead said. 'It wouldn't have made any difference anyway.'

Pauline suggested they could have mobilised more support. The other two reminded her of the glowing letters she'd got from commissioners, their healthy financial forecast and the savings they'd already implemented. The three of them had worked tirelessly to prevent Appelby from being closed.

'Remember the two board members who told you it would be fine?' Marcus asked. 'You had no way of knowing the bastards would throw us under the bus and vote to shut us down.'

Pauline shook her head. 'I kidded myself. I allowed myself to hope. I got your hopes up too.'

We looked towards the ceiling at the sound of screaming from upstairs. 'Do we need to step in?' Marcus asked. We waited. It stopped.

'I keep thinking about my dad,' Pauline continued. 'He lost his job when I was sixteen. Mum never forgave him. She thought he'd failed to see the writing on the wall. Her bitterness infected everything. Eventually he got another job he loved. But the family changed forever. Dad's shame shrank him. He became smaller.' She pulled at her earlobe repeatedly.

Sinead shifted in her seat. 'Pauline, you can't blame yourself. You did everything possible.'

'No.' Pauline shook her head. 'When they sold the

premises, I thought that would be it and we'd be OK. I should have known better.'

I said I hadn't seen it coming either; that with all the support for Appelby and their consistently brilliant inspection reports, I'd thought it would work out. Maybe we'd all turned a blind eye.

The day before our next session with the team, Pauline rang me again. She'd had an anonymous letter from one of the staff blaming her for the closure. The writer hadn't found a job, didn't know how they'd feed their family and claimed that Pauline didn't care – about Appelby or any of them. Three words ended the note: 'You destroyed us.'

'I'm sorry,' I said. 'That's horrible.' We agreed that given closure, what mattered now wasn't disciplining the letter writer, but surfacing and understanding what the letter expressed for the whole team.

I arrived early for the session. When Pauline told them about the letter, the intake of breath reverberated through the packed room. Everyone looked around. Eyes met briefly before averting swiftly to study shoes, chair legs, the gap between the rug and the door. Throats were cleared. Someone jumped up to open a window. The unspoken question hung in the air: '*Was it you?*'

I thought of the custody battle over the girl who'd tried to kill herself. At this moment, the team were in danger of succumbing to destructiveness and pulling apart like those parents. Under continued stress, their drive towards death had strengthened and snatched the upper hand over their life drive. I said we needed to think about what the letter represented, not who wrote it. Presumably others, not only the writer, felt angry and let down. Pauline confirmed that she wasn't searching out a 'culprit' and wouldn't discipline anyone.

For a moment I saw confusion, perhaps disappointment as

the thrill of the hunt abated. A nurse spoke up. 'I know it's not your fault,' she said to Pauline. 'I know you did all you could, but somewhere I'm really angry.'

'This place has meant so much to me,' a psychologist said. 'I refused to think any of this could be down to you. I feel let down though. Couldn't you have stopped this? Really?' Her voice caught as she pushed back tears. 'I didn't know I felt that.'

Neil mentioned the staff who'd already left. He'd thought they were selfish but now wondered if they'd done the right thing. 'Why am I staying on a sinking ship?'

'Because of the children,' Helen replied.

'What about me?' Neil asked.

Pauline told them they all needed to put themselves first and find other jobs.

The sound of children's footsteps drifted into the quiet stillness of the room.

'Why didn't you tell us about closing down sooner?' Neil asked gently.

'We hoped we could prevent it and didn't want to upset you unnecessarily,' Sinead replied. 'I don't know if that was right. Do you?' She looked at Pauline and Marcus.

'No, I don't,' Marcus said.

'I thought so at the time, but now I have no idea,' Pauline acknowledged.

I felt admiration as well as tenderness towards them. I've rarely come across leaders so open and honest, and so willing to show their uncertainty and vulnerability to their staff.

'This was my first job after qualifying as a psychotherapist,' Helen said. 'I've learnt an extraordinary amount. I can't believe they're closing us down. In a stroke. After everything we've built up here.' She looked at the leaders. 'After all you've put in. OK, the company doesn't give a toss about us, but what about the children? They're so vulnerable.'

A nurse wiped away her tears. 'I haven't found another job. What if I don't fit in anywhere else? I dread working somewhere with less care and commitment to the children.'

'I started here a month after Pauline ten years ago,' Sinead murmured. 'I love what we've made of this place. The end of Appelby makes me weep.'

I held back my own tears. In that slow moment, it dawned on me that my work with the team had changed: it was no longer about their communication and dynamics. I had to accompany them during the last few months and help them hold onto their life drive until Appelby's death.

At a time when many leaders would think my sessions pointless and reduce them, Pauline asked me to increase them. I did more sessions with the staff and we also agreed to have another meeting with the senior team.

Back in the small room with the three of them again, the sputter of a lawnmower engine interrupted us. Sinead, waving to the gardener, sighed. 'I'm sick of being so bloody nice and understanding, and always supporting the team. They're not that supportive to us right now.'

Pauline nodded. 'People whinged at me yesterday. I wanted to wring their necks. Don't they understand I don't have the time for every niggle?'

'You want the team to think about you and your needs now, not just their own. Hopefully, sometimes they can, but in a way why should they? You're the bosses and they're losing their jobs. Who else are they going to take it out on?' I asked.

'How about no one?' Sinead said.

Our laugher released the tension.

'You're right of course,' Pauline said, looking at me. 'But it's still hard being understanding all the time.'

I nodded. 'It's hard to keep hold of love for the staff and children when you're being closed down.'

'Too bloody right,' Marcus said.

When I arrived at Appelby for the last time, Pauline met me at reception, just as she had on my first visit in the old building. Dressed from head to foot in dark navy, she looked as if she was going to a funeral. I was glad I'd changed from black to a yellow dress before leaving home. People had returned early from their holidays and the night shift workers, who I'd never met, had come along for the first time. We made our way to a different room, as we couldn't all fit in our normal meeting space. They'd arranged their goodbye lunch straight afterwards.

I hadn't expected my session to be Appelby's last ever meeting, yet it made sense. I'd witnessed their journey, now they needed me to witness their death.

All the children had gone. The last to leave was the girl who'd attempted suicide. They hadn't been able to find an alternative service for her. Although she'd made great progress and her parents had continued therapy and dropped the custody battle, the team knew that leaving treatment prematurely increased the risk of her deteriorating.

'You've all done an amazing job finding the right places for most of the children and supporting their parents,' Pauline said.

'You helped us keep going up to the very end.' Neil looked at the senior team.

'You all kept hope – yours, and the patients and parents' – alive,' I said.

They recalled events, both painful and funny, and talked about their plans for after Appelby. I listened to the melody of emotions: sadness, appreciation, affection, anger and joy. I recognised the quiet battle between their life-affirming constructiveness and their destructiveness. And, despite Appelby's death, I heard their indomitable life drive claim ascendency.

As I said my goodbyes to them, the staff unpacked the food they'd brought in. The large table overflowed with dishes from their many different cultures. A little bit of each of them woven together in an abundance of smells and colours.

4

Another Side of Aggression

It was already 10.15 a.m. I shut the door of my consulting room and went upstairs.

When we'd talked on the phone and arranged the 10 a.m. session, Bilal said his wife had suggested coaching because of his stress. Aged forty-seven, he'd worked in human resources at the same international food manufacturing company for seventeen years. For the last year, he'd led a company-wide, well-being project and, ironically, taken more sick leave than in his entire career.

Tapping away at my computer, the doorbell startled me. I checked my watch: 10.30. A small grey man stood on the doorstep in the bright spring sunshine. Grey hair, grey skin, a grey suit. He looked older than his years. Bilal tentatively offered his hand, withdrew it, then fumbled, before briefly shaking my extended hand.

'I'm sorry,' he said. 'I went the wrong way. Stupid of me. Sorry.' He shifted uncomfortably.

'Don't worry, you're here now.' I ushered him inside. 'Do you want to leave your rucksack here?' I gestured to the coat stand in the hall.

'Oh, yes, thank you. Maybe I'll leave my jacket too.' He hunched his shoulders, beginning to take it off, but his hand got caught in the left sleeve. 'I'll just keep it on,' he said. 'I'm a bit cold, anyway.'

I noticed his pale lips, red eyes, and puffy face. Coughing, he rummaged for a handkerchief and blew his nose.

'A cold?' I asked, pointing him towards my consulting room.

'It's been one thing after another. Coughs, allergies, stomach problems. A bad back.'

Squeezing himself into the corner of the sofa, Bilal cast a furtive look around the room. His eyes flitted across the fireplace opposite, the chaise longue in the corner next to a large bookcase, the deep orange sofa I sat on at a right angle to him. Checking twice that it wouldn't be too much trouble, he asked for a coffee.

'Perhaps I just need to pull myself together,' he said, when I returned with our drinks. 'I'm not sure my wife's right about stress. It's such an overused word.'

Shrinking further into the sofa, Bilal pressed one thumb into the palm of his other hand. He told me he couldn't sleep, had awful eczema and was constantly irritated. 'I wake up every day with a terrible sinking feeling – dread – about going to work.'

I asked what he dreaded.

He studied the vase of yellow tulips on the mantelpiece. A car horn sounded outside. He chewed his bottom lip. 'Everything.'

Walking me through his day of meetings, progress reports and planning, he explained that although his new role was a promotion, his grade hadn't changed, yet his workload had doubled. As well as running the well-being project, he continued to perform his old role of managing a team of human resource officers.

At the outset of the project people were excited because it was the first initiative to bring line managers, the unions and human resources together. But the team members had to fit the project around their regular work, so kept missing milestones.

'People have lost faith,' he said gloomily. 'They thought things would really change. So far we've just gathered information.'

I asked why more hadn't happened.

'Because I've messed up. I've made one bad call after another.'

He ticked them off on his fingers: putting decisions off until it was too late; not prioritising or getting the priorities wrong; not protecting the team from the pressure, but at the same time letting them push him around. He took a gulp of coffee.

At the team meeting the day before, people complained about the shortage of time for discussion. At their request, he'd reduced the number of meetings, but now they ran out of time and rushed the agenda without properly considering important items. He'd told them to prepare for the meetings, but no one did. They didn't even read the agenda beforehand. He'd given up.

'I told you I'm no good at this.' He rubbed his palm against the side of his trousers.

I suggested that the company must have seen something in him to give him the job.

'Maybe I'm just the guy who won't complain. The one who puts up and shuts up.'

'Are you?'

'Probably. I don't like confrontation.'

'Standing up for yourself is confrontation?'

He shrugged, trying again to take his jacket off. He folded it carefully and put it down next to him. 'Usually. And that's aggressive.'

'Perhaps you see aggression as only bad and destructive, not in any way positive,' I said.

'Aggression *is* negative. There is no positive sense.'

I realised we'd reached the nub of Bilal's problem. A leader who's scared of aggression – either their own or other people's – is in trouble. He needed to mobilise his aggression healthily. Instead, he put up with an impossible situation, complained about his workload and the project team's behaviour, but did nothing about it. And all the time his stress got worse.

Looking towards the door, Bilal asked if he could use the toilet. When he returned, he told me that I kept calling him *project leader* when his title was *project coordinator.*

'Sorry. I'm glad you corrected me. But you are the project leader, aren't you?'

'Well, yes. It's just a title. But I thought I should point that out. It's no big thing. Forget I mentioned it.'

'No, I'm glad you mentioned it. I do think it's a big thing that you have overall accountability for the project's success, but no resources or authority over the team. You said no one listens to you. I suspect your title may contribute to that.'

'It's just a word.'

'So why not call you "project leader"?'

'I am the leader. I'm just called coordinator.'

I said that a coordinator usually pulls things together but doesn't have the authority to lead.

A moment passed. Bilal put his head in his hands. 'I don't even believe in the project anymore. I did, passionately, but now . . . I don't think I do. I don't believe in the company or in my job. I'm not even sure why I'm here.' His voice, like his body, drooped with despondency.

I registered depression as well as stress. Depression that I suspected resulted from him unconsciously avoiding his feelings of anger and aggression towards others and turning them against himself.

Sitting on the edge of the sofa, eyes fixed firmly on his feet, he reminded me of a trapped animal about to bolt. I realised I'd sighed without meaning to when he suddenly looked across at me. 'It seems your hands are tied behind your back the whole time,' I said.

His eyes focused on mine. He swallowed. 'I don't think I can do it anymore.' We sat in silence.

'I am stressed, aren't I?' he asked.

'Yes, you are. Perhaps a bit depressed too?'

'It's hard to admit – even to myself.'

I nodded.

'But not all the problems are down to me?'

'No, they're not.'

'I don't know why we got stuck on the job title,' he said after a while. 'It doesn't matter. Sorry about that.'

It seemed the right moment to explore Bilal's lack of authority further. 'Have you thought that the project, and you as its coordinator, could have been set up to fail?'

Alarm spread across his face. 'How? Why? That doesn't make sense.'

'That's what we need to understand. Could the company have fudged things by calling you "coordinator" instead of "leader"?'

'If that's true . . . but I don't think it is. They're not like that.'

'It may not have been conscious.'

'Even so.'

'You're angry that they may have set you up?' I asked.

He leaned back. 'Yes. I suppose I am. But what good does getting angry do?'

'Loads of good sometimes.'

'Oh, yeah. Aggression. I told you, I don't do that.'

Bilal had got into a similar situation in his last job at another company, when he'd unquestioningly taken on an impossible role and ill-conceived project. Then, as now, he'd felt a failure and ashamed. The feelings went back to his school days. He told me that his father always teased him. If Bilal got an 'A' for his homework, his dad would say pity it wasn't an 'A+'. When Bilal stood up for himself, saying that an 'A' was really good, his dad would say he couldn't take a joke. 'He pretended not to mind when I failed the eleven-plus, but I knew he did.'

Bilal's dad couldn't go to university because the family needed him to work. Bilal's paternal grandfather had treated his dad with condescension, laughing at his opinions, as though he was stupid. Bilal remembered his grandad criticising everything: the way his father talked, the way he walked, dressed, his choice of books.

'Dad became very bitter over the years,' Bilal said. 'I think it was because in his eyes he never achieved enough.'

'You thought you had to make up for that?'

'We all did. It was OK for my brothers and sisters because they did really well in school and in their jobs. But I always failed.'

I wondered how his sense of failure affected the situation at work. I asked if he'd ever talked to his boss about his job title and authority. He said he couldn't, because he hadn't achieved enough. In fact, he should probably apologise for not getting further.

'Bilal . . .' I broke off.

'That was the wrong answer, wasn't it?' he said.

My irritation instantly subsided. We both laughed.

As the session drew to a close, I suggested we meet his boss together as part of setting up coaching so that she could support it as an integral component of his development.

'I often do that,' I said. 'You could raise the issue of

authority and your job title as part of discussing your goals for coaching.'

The colour drained from his face. 'Oh God no. Meeting her together would be like ganging up on her.'

I said that on the contrary, surely she needed to know that the current set-up meant he couldn't lead properly, and the project couldn't succeed, but he was adamant.

Over the weekend my email pinged.

'I'm really sorry,' Bilal wrote, 'but I need to cancel Wednesday's session. I've decided to look for a new job. Until then I'm going to take up swimming again and acupuncture to help me relax. Thank you very much for everything.'

I replied on Monday morning saying it was fine to stop coaching and to get in touch if he ever wanted another session, or just a telephone conversation. I didn't try to persuade him to return. It was his decision, even if I thought it was a bad one.

On Thursday morning, while I was enjoying a double espresso in my favourite café, my mobile rang. 'Sorry to bother you,' Bilal said, 'but could I possibly see you again?' We arranged a session for late Tuesday afternoon.

Arriving right on time, Bilal looked strained and tired. He told me he'd been thinking about aggression. He realised his children had been aggressive from a very young age. As little ones they kicked, pulled hair and tried to bite Bilal and his wife and each other given half the chance. Later at school, aggression flourished in name-calling and fighting in the playground.

'The psychoanalyst Melanie Klein wrote about that,' I told him. 'Our ubiquitous capacity for aggression starts very early in life.'

The tension eased from Bilal's face. 'It's normal then?'

'Yes,' I said. 'It takes aggression for toddlers to muster the willpower and determination to move on their own, to talk and start to become their own person.'

We talked about how hard, impossible, it had been for Bilal to use the ordinary aggression adolescents need to find their own identity, to separate from and succeed their parents.

'You came to see me the first time at your wife's suggestion,' I said. 'I wasn't sure if you agreed or just went along with her.'

'I went along with her,' he replied.

I asked him how he stood up to her when he disagreed with her.

'I tell her to listen to me,' he said, sitting upright, 'that just because my opinion is different, it doesn't mean it's wrong.'

'Can you do that at work?'

'Maybe.' He leaned forward. 'Something's just crystallised: Dad tortured himself with fear of failure. Maybe without realising it, I became the disappointing one in the family to relieve him of some of that.'

The pain of the unspoken, unconscious family script allotting Bilal the role of the disappointing failure sat in the room with us. He breathed slowly. 'I'm still stressed and not sleeping,' he said. 'Perhaps the stress and disappointment go together.' He decided it was time to overcome his fear and enlist his boss Charmian's support. He was ready to try the meeting with her I'd suggested.

Two weeks later, they arrived together. Bilal said his main goal for coaching was to improve the way he led the project. Charmian told him he already led it well, that he was sensitive, collaborative and cared about people. She hesitated, glanced at me, but said no more. Bilal looked at me, before replying.

'Thanks, but it doesn't feel like I'm doing well.' He looked over Charmian's shoulder. 'I find it hard to use my authority. We're working on that in these sessions.'

'Really? Well, I suppose you sometimes let the team push you around a bit. It would be great if coaching can help with that. And what can I do to support you with it?'

'Actually ...'

Charmian interrupted. 'The senior team and the board are watching the project closely.' She leaned forward. 'It's an urgent priority this year. I can't say much, but there've been some mental health issues and people are worried. They're finally taking well-being seriously.'

Bilal caught my eye. Coughing, his words tumbled out: 'Actually I'm not coping too well.'

Charmian looked dismayed. He reassured her he wasn't going to do anything stupid, but he found leading the project stressful. That was why he kept getting ill and having time off. He hadn't told her, because he thought he should be able to sort it out for himself.

'The stress felt like a weakness, a failure,' he said.

'I had no idea,' Charmian said. 'Why don't you go on a course, do some management training? Look up what appeals to you. I'll fund it.'

'It's not about training,' Bilal said. 'There's no time or people for the project—'

'Well that's true up to a point but—'

'It *is* true. And I'm meant to lead the project but I'm the coordinator. I don't have the authority to lead.'

'Come on, Bilal.' Charmian's tone changed. 'You can't expect authority to be handed to you on a plate. You have to take it. You could have at least talked to me about this. I gave you plenty of openings.'

'You say that as if telling you I'm not coping and dread work so much that I could barely get out of bed some days, is easy,' Bilal said, looking her straight in the eye.

Charmian broke eye contact. Neither of them spoke. The clock ticked quietly.

'I'm sorry,' Charmian said, looking at Bilal again. 'I think of myself as approachable. It's not as simple as that, is it? And you're right about the project. Your role is ambiguous. Instead of clarifying it, we relied on your goodwill.'

'Thank you for acknowledging that. I know I've contributed to this, but I'm determined to change things now. I have to.'

'You both have to,' I said.

'Yes,' Bilal said. 'Otherwise, the project will fail.'

He told Charmian they had to resolve the company's conflicting wishes for well-being with the steering group that oversaw the project. And she had to give him what he needed to lead it. They agreed he'd take proper time off and they'd meet with the steering group when he returned. In the meantime, Charmian would make the case for resourcing the project appropriately and making Bilal its director.

I was proud of Bilal. Less fearful of his aggression, he'd started using it healthily. He'd found authority not just from his role, but from within himself. He'd used it to stand up to Charmian. He'd even let himself get cross.

An enlivened and bolder Bilal had emerged from his former grey shadow.

5

The Looking Glass

After two sessions with the managers of a university careers service, I suggested a workshop with the whole team.

'I'm not sure that's a good idea,' Carol, head of the service, said, a faint pulse throbbing below her right eye. Mid-fifties, with greying hair and sensible clothes, she gave the impression of having long since given up on fun and frivolity.

'It's not,' Toby, her deputy, agreed. He was a few years younger than Carol; short, squat and just the right side of scruffy.

Roshana and Beatrice, the other two members of the senior team, were in their first management jobs. Roshana reminded me that half the team weren't speaking to them and the other half were rude and aggressive.

Beatrice picked a loose thread in the sleeve of her cardigan. 'I don't think I can. I can't do a workshop.'

I registered the fear and panic in the room.

They talked about how difficult higher education had become, how much it had changed and the impact of funding cuts. Within the service, they'd been under the intense pressure of performance managing two of the staff, who'd eventually resigned. Not being allowed to say anything about it to the team made it much harder. They couldn't even counter the stories staff spread. That it was Carol's fault, she was a terrible manager and had it in for the two that left. They were, I realised, frightened of their staff.

'We'll only do a workshop if and when you're ready,' I reassured them.

At our next session they decided to go ahead.

Two weeks before the workshop, I had a one and a half hour meeting with the staff to hear their perspective. Although they were initially suspicious – what would I report back to the managers? – they gradually opened up. The managers, they said, bullied, criticised, lied. They micromanaged, were inconsistent and offered zero support to staff. They blamed everyone else for their mistakes and didn't understand the most basic aspects of a university careers service. They questioned staff about the quality of their work and ticked them off about their timekeeping and record keeping. As if it mattered, when the important thing was helping students get started on their career.

The litany slowed; voices petered out. 'And . . .' someone said.

People looked at one another. A man nodded at Maggs, a tall woman with a blonde quiff through her dark hair. She sat forward, rubbing her cheekbone as she spoke. 'The managers have got rid of staff,' she said. 'With no good reason. Maliciously. We never know who will be next. The message is clear though: step out of line and you're gone.'

'It makes us all feel paranoid,' John added. The longest-serving member of the team, he was older than the others.

Were they talking about the same managers I'd met? The managers who'd struck me as warm, competent, and caring leaders? They'd been open about their struggles and vulnerability. I liked them. I'd thought they were the victims, not the perpetrators, of bullying. Had I mis-seen them? Got them completely wrong? Had they duped me?

John carefully straightened his tie. He described the caustic comments the managers made if you spent a few extra minutes in the kitchen talking to your colleagues. 'No wonder you're behind with your record keeping,' they'd say, or 'I'm surprised you've got time for chatter.' A veiled threat about disciplinary action frequently followed these jibes.

I glanced at my watch – 11.30. Our meeting finished at noon. The anger and contempt towards the managers showed no sign of abating. Why had I suggested a workshop? The managers were right: it was a bad idea.

'I don't agree,' a young, fair-haired man, Konrad, said, his Polish accent breaking into my reverie. 'The managers do understand the work of the department. I think they're OK.'

A woman agreed; the senior team weren't all bad. It was a chink of light in the haze of hostility.

'Maybe we should forget the workshops and take a grievance against the managers,' Maggs said, tossing back her blonde quiff. Cries of assent rang around the room. Konrad's attempt to turn the team away from their wish to fight the managers had failed. In the teams' minds, the managers remained unremittingly bad. The momentary light went out and my hope somersaulted to the pit of my stomach.

'You think it's totally hopeless?' I asked.

'Completely,' Maggs said. 'The managers can't be trusted. Not for a moment.'

'We can't just give up,' Konrad said.

Hope inched up again, like a spirit level moving a few millimetres towards equilibrium. I knew I needed to grab it and build on the difference in opinion they were voicing, suggesting a slight loosening of the glue sticking them so tightly together. Maybe they could now edge their way towards being a group of individuals, rather than an undifferentiated gang. I invited them to think about the state of mind they needed to be in for the workshop to stand a chance of success.

Konrad suggested they take the managers as they found them rather than seeing them through the lens of everything that had happened before. Others agreed. Maggs said they mustn't hold back about their own feelings. I suspected she was telling the team, and perhaps warning me, that she wouldn't spare the managers any of her derision. But with time running out, I chose to take the ambiguity of her words positively. Yes, I said, being as honest as they could about what things were like for them, while remaining open to the managers' experience, was vital. I left feeling more optimistic.

The next day I met the managers again, to help them prepare for the workshop.

'We know the knives will be out for us,' Roshana said.

'They probably won't talk,' Beatrice added.

'Certainly won't listen,' Roshana agreed.

'Whatever happens, I don't believe anything will change,' Carol said, tears welling in her eyes.

'We have to believe it can,' Toby rallied.

'Do we? For how long?' Roshana asked. 'Isn't it better to be realistic?'

'I think you do believe it can change, however fragile that belief is,' I said. 'You wouldn't have got me in otherwise, and we wouldn't be doing the workshop.'

They moved their heads in the smallest of nods, their faces bleak. They would go into the workshop positively, they said, suspend history and try to be open, not defensive. They smiled bravely at me as we said goodbye.

I felt as if I'd explained to a group of children the pain involved in an operation they were about to endure, one that may or may not work, and left them anxious and alone to wait for the dreaded hour.

On the day of the workshop, it poured relentlessly. My umbrella bobbed above my head as I lowered and raised it, trying to avoid stabbing people on the crowded pavements between the tube and the university.

The gloomy grey light lent a foreboding air to the enormous room. I went from window to window, pulling up the blinds. At the other end of the blank space the administrator finished putting out crisps, cupcakes, a bowl of fruit and an assortment of biscuits, tea, coffee and fruit juices. 'I thought we might need these.' She smiled at me.

She helped me arrange twenty-five blue plastic chairs, some new and pristine, some scratched and stained, in a large circle. People wandered in and headed to the table of drinks and snacks. Snippets of hushed conversation drifted over to me: '. . . keep our cool . . .', 'don't be fooled', '. . . do this for Becky.' Becky, I remembered, was one of the staff who'd resigned rather than facing a disciplinary for poor performance.

Heads bent together, they sat in small groups talking intensely and scribbling on flip chart paper. I'd asked the managers to identify what incorrect assumptions they thought staff made about them and vice versa. I invited the groups to feed back.

'You never said we'd have to do that,' John complained.

Another man excused himself to go to the toilet; a woman coughed, and people clucked around her, offering cough sweets and bringing her water. I wondered if covering over anxiety in this way was part of the team culture.

'You think we're lazy and incompetent,' Maggs said, looking at the managers. 'That we take short cuts and don't care about our work. You don't trust us.'

'You think we don't care about the students,' someone else added.

'Hang on—' Konrad tried.

'And that we skive and deliberately withhold information from you,' John interrupted.

I raised my eyebrows encouragingly at the managers. Beatrice stared into the middle distance, tapping her forefinger and thumb together.

'We think you don't trust us either,' Carol said.

'You think we're totally incompetent,' Roshana added.

'And only see mistakes in your work,' Toby said. 'That we constantly look for mistakes.'

'You assume we make life hard for you deliberately and are out to get you,' Carol continued, a tremor in her voice.

'But—' John started. He stopped, shaking his head.

'You're surprised by the similarity?' I asked. John nodded slowly. Others muttered in agreement.

'They *do* get it,' Konrad said.

'Of course we bloody do,' Toby replied angrily. 'We're not stupid.'

'You seem determined to see us as Machiavellian villains,' Carol said.

'And stupid,' Toby reiterated.

The door opened and a man strode in before backing out, his armed raised apologetically, when he saw us.

'Sometimes it's hard for me to come to work in the morning,' Roshana admitted tearfully. 'I'm trying my best. I make mistakes, I know I do, but whatever I do, to you I'm always useless and malicious. I can't change how you see me.'

I caught Beatrice's eye. She cleared her throat. 'It's like . . . it's like . . . body dysmorphia. I see one thing when I look in the mirror, but you see something completely different.'

The rain pounded against the windows. Tension and misery shot through their faces. 'We've really put you in a box, seen you through a distorted lens, haven't we,' Maggs said. 'Like *Alice Through the Looking Glass*.' She wiped her tears with the end of her sleeve.

'Maybe we've done the same to you,' Carol replied. 'It's topsy-turvy; we all see everything the opposite way around.'

They told each other how they actually felt about their work and the service. As they talked and listened, the mis-shapen ghouls and monsters turned into ordinary people with strengths and flaws. Ordinary people doing their best in organisational stress and difficulty. We agreed to have a second workshop a month later.

The rain had finally stopped. On the tube home, my mind drifted, lulled by the sway of the carriage as it rumbled across the city. I thought of *Alice Through the Looking Glass* again and the peculiar looking glass of our minds. We turn things upside down and round about because we find it so hard to integrate our paradoxical selves – to accept the ghouls, along with the heroes and heroines, as part of us. And, when we can't bear to know a part of ourselves, whether good or bad, our unconscious cleverly projects it out. Like breaking off mould from the edge of a block of cheese and chucking it away. Except that the mould isn't only on the outer edges; its tentacles spread throughout the rest of the cheese. We often take a further unconscious step and inject it into someone else, without them knowing. Then, peering through our inside-out looking glass, we see mould all over them.

I remembered a team in a medium secure forensic unit for sex offenders with learning difficulties who'd projected their anxiety – injected their mould – about being useless and incompetent, into their manager. They behaved towards her almost as though she too had learning disabilities, helping the projections take hold and join with her own self-doubt. She flailed around, making mistakes, which confirmed the team's distorted image of her.

Without knowing it, they also used projection to communicate with me. After one session, I felt utterly depressed and despairing and wept uncontrollably when I got home. Later, I understood that the team had projected some of their pain and despair about their patients into me. It both spared them from this and, by giving me a taste of their experience, generated my empathy and understanding.

The tube juddered to a stop. Projecting out unbearable parts of our selves is ordinary, I reminded myself, especially when we're anxious. And it's normal for staff to project into their managers; our bosses unconsciously trigger feelings about our parents, who, for most of us, were our first authority figures. In the careers service, the projection wasn't just between individuals, but between groups. Again, not uncommon. There are always reasons though; I needed to work out what the team and managers found unbearable. And why projection was their only way of dealing with it.

A month later, a gaggle of students dawdled, laughing together outside the building. As I got near, I saw a tall girl with vivid pink hair, velvet plum shorts, Bobber boots and the words 'Pink Freud' on her T-shirt. I thought of the work the service did, helping young people full of life, energy and hope, and considerable anxiety, too, as they embarked on careers or simply tried to get jobs that would reward their hard work and student loans.

The spread of cakes and biscuits, fruit and juices loaded the table again. The blinds had already been pulled up. Laughter and chatter made the room seem less cavernous. The team told me things had improved between them. It wasn't great, but the staff and managers could mostly talk to each other without descending into antagonism.

I said I'd been thinking about Alice's looking glass and the powerful, unconscious mechanism of projection. I wondered if this was what distorted their looking glass. We put the pieces together: the state of the university and students and, in this context, the position of the careers service. Through images, metaphors and words they painted a picture of a cut-off, arrogant senior leadership team in the university, a vulnerable careers service and highly anxious students.

'Uni isn't how it used to be – how it was for us. Now students have huge loans to pay back and massive competition for jobs,' Maggs said.

'Before a 2:2 was fine; now a 2:1 is only just OK. They all want a first, so they'll get a good job and make the loans or large sums given by their parents worthwhile,' John added.

A team member who hadn't yet spoken said that one of the counsellors had told him that almost all the students are on antidepressants at one time or another during their degree, especially in their final year.

'Jesus. That's terrible.' Roshana raised her arms. 'What the hell's going on?'

'It's a shocking indictment of anxiety in higher education, and the way antidepressants get dished out so readily,' I said. 'If the students are that anxious, no wonder they project some of it into you.'

'I wonder what the figures are for staff,' Konrad muttered.

'Loads of people are off with stress,' John said. 'The university doesn't know what to do about it. Human resources offer mindfulness, but it's aimed at individuals, as though the stress is our fault because we're not resilient. Makes me sick. What about the fact that workloads have become impossible and that everyone is under stupid amounts of pressure?'

I suggested this made it more likely for staff to also turn to projection.

Perhaps helped by the space the workshop had opened up, Maggs asked about the two staff who'd left. 'I know both of them were off with stress at various times, but then they disappeared. The union said you'd got rid of them.'

'We can't talk about it,' Carol said. 'It's confidential. I know that makes it hard. It's hard for us too. But I'm sure you wouldn't want us to say anything if it was you.'

I couldn't gauge whether staff heard this as one of the veiled threats they'd talked about, as though Carol was saying it could be one of them next.

'"Getting rid of them" sounds as though you believe we're heartless and malicious,' Toby commented. No one responded.

John shifted in his seat. 'How can we trust you when people vanish like that? Especially since the two of them said you were always on at them and wanted them out.'

'We can't talk about it,' Carol repeated firmly.

The coffee break brought some relief. People milled around munching crisps, chatting to each other. After the break they talked more about the students.

A young woman mentioned a particularly worrying student she was seeing. 'He's bipolar. He's had a really hard time getting to the third year – took a year off at one point – but he's done it which is amazing. I'm scared of saying anything that will put him back though.'

'Are you talking about the student we discussed yesterday?' Beatrice asked.

'Yes.'

'Remember he's being seen by the counselling service too. Your job is to help him with his career, not his mental health.'

'They can't always be separated. Surely this student should have been allocated to a senior advisor?' Maggs straightened her back as she resumed her hidden role as gang leader which the team and she herself, had unconsciously allotted to her.

'We didn't know about the mental health problems when we allocated him,' Carol explained.

'That happens a lot,' Beatrice said. 'You're never left alone with these difficult cases though. We always support you.' The young woman nodded.

'I do know that,' Maggs acknowledged. 'Sorry. I go straight to blame, don't I?' She and the managers exchanged smiles.

We thought about the students blaming the careers advisors, seeing them as useless, if they failed to find a good job or their perfect career. Perhaps students projected uselessness and blame into the advisors to avoid blaming themselves for the failure they felt by letting down their parents, just as the staff and managers blamed each other.

'I don't always care about the students in the way I should,' Maggs said. 'There's one I'm seeing at the moment. She drives me crazy. Nothing I do is right. I'm so pleased if she cancels.' She looked at the managers. 'That's when I spend more time in the kitchen – after seeing her.'

'That's fair enough,' Toby said. 'We're too quick to blame, too.'

I'd reread some of *Alice's Adventures in Wonderland* the night before and walking back to the tube after the workshop, Alice's words came back to me: 'I know who I *was* when I got up this morning, but I think I must have been changed several times since then.'

She might have said, I know who I *was* and who those around me were, but I think I must have changed the lenses in my glasses several times since then.

I thought of the stress and distress the staff and managers had caused each other by looking through glass smeared with their assumptions and misbeliefs and how often I come across that in organisations. The array of glasses we all use in and out of work: the ones that bring reality into focus and the ones that blur it. And how the distortion of these lenses affects our responses and the sense we make of other people and the world.

6

Barriers and Barricades

'I've got a body on the table in fifteen minutes,' the surgeon said, bringing our phone call to an abrupt end. His words hit me: how could he describe a patient so coldly? But his expression came from defensiveness, not a lack of feeling.

Working with surgeons taught me how vital our psychological defences are to organisational life. They couldn't do their jobs without sufficient emotional armour. They wouldn't be able to cut open, injure and risk killing their patients. Talking about a 'body on the table' kept the patient at a necessary psychological distance. Before or after surgery, the surgeons referred to patients by name; they were people. For the operation though, patients became blood, flesh, organs and body parts.

While the life and death nature of a surgeon's work makes their defences particularly important, we all rely on them. Mostly unconscious, they provide a protective barrier that helps us cope with the inherent difficulties of living – both the difficulties in our minds and in the external world. Internally our defences alleviate the terror of our mortality. They help us keep our fears in check – about our destructive qualities such as our cynicism and hatred, and also our constructive qualities such as love and the difficult feelings of dependency and jealousy it often provokes.

The surgeons had asked me in because of problems in their team. I soon understood the importance of leaving their defences intact. Yet, I knew that to stand a chance of shifting the entrenched patterns between them, they'd have to let their guard down. The line between allowing enough to get across their defensive layer, while maintaining sufficient protection, was delicate and, at times, unstable.

Courageously, over the course of our sessions, the surgeons began showing their vulnerability to me, each other and to themselves. The agony and guilt of a near mistake for instance, the pain of ageing and beginning to lose dexterity. Once though, one of them told me our conversation made him feel ill and he now had to perform a high-risk operation on an extremely sick patient. I lay awake that night. What if the patient died because I'd breached the surgeon's defences, rendering him unable to operate safely? Eventually, I realised I'd absorbed some of the anxiety he'd unconsciously projected into me. Hopefully this enabled him to restore his defences and become sufficiently omnipotent to do his job.

To varying extents and at different times, we all use omnipotence as a defence against our vulnerability and helplessness. And we all split off parts of ourselves, other people and the world. We reduce uncertainty by creating false, simplistic divisions: people are good or bad, with us or against us; the world is divided into developed and undeveloped parts; complex political and economic issues are reduced to catchy phrases.

We also commonly use the defences of denial, idealisation, control and repression. At a global level many of us have long denied climate change rather than face the terrifying truth. Every day we may deny an addiction, poor leadership or low staff morale. We may idealise people to stave off our anxiety and disappointment in their essential flaws. We try to control or suppress our own frightening thoughts and feelings and try to control others to avoid anxiety about our lack of control over them.

Each of us also develops and uses defences in different ways. One of my clients, whose parents were highly envious of him, learnt to use failure as a defence against his fear of success; another intellectualised to stop herself feeling. The aloofness another client displayed defended against intimacy.

We create defences in our organisations too. They become part of the organisation's culture, its DNA, forming an unconscious collective protection. This helps maintain equilibrium, but if the protective barrier of our defences, the skin of our emotional world, becomes a barricade, our workplaces are in trouble.

On 28 January 1986, the space shuttle *Challenger* exploded seventy-three seconds after lift-off. On 1 February 2003, after re-entering the earth's atmosphere, the space shuttle *Columbia* exploded thirty-eight miles above the ground, sixteen minutes before landing. Both of these fatal events were preventable.

The Rogers Commission investigation into *Challenger* found that the explosion was caused by a design fault in the solid rocket booster joint and seal. But, they said, the disaster wasn't only down to technical failings: failures in communication and decision-making also played a part.

Technical issues had delayed *Challenger*'s launch twice, so senior leaders were particularly keen that nothing should stop it this time. They hadn't been told about recent problems with the joint and seal. Neither did they know of the row between staff at NASA and a contractor the evening before *Challenger* launched: the predicted low temperature meant there was a danger of ice on the launch pad and the contractor wanted to postpone the launch. The crew didn't know about this either.

They weren't told at weather discussions or at the weather briefing on the morning of lift-off.

'If the decision-makers had known all of the facts,' the Rogers Commission said, 'it is highly unlikely that they would have decided to launch.'

In 2003, *Columbia* disintegrated because a piece of foam fell off the external fuel tank 81.7 seconds after lift-off and breached the left wing. The Columbia Accident Investigation Board (CAIB) concluded that 'organisational system failure' had once again critically affected how risk increased, was defined, and ignored. NASA, they said, hadn't learnt from *Challenger*; they'd normalised risk and ignored external advice.

Dismissing external advice suggests both omnipotence and grandiosity. This turns an organisational barrier into a barricade that prevents anything getting through. The barricade causes insufficient contact with, and a distortion of reality, so impeding learning and change.

In some sense we all contributed to NASA's barricade. Since 20 July 1969, when Neil Armstrong walked on the moon, the space agency symbolised science at the edge of miracles. The CAIB suggested that the achievement of landing a man on the moon and the subsequent accolades reinforced staff's idealised image of NASA as a 'perfect place', as 'the best organization that human beings could create to accomplish selected goals'.

Rather than thinking about criticism from contractors or the Rogers Commission, NASA turned inwards. In *Perfect Places: NASA as an Idealized Institution* (1989), Garry D. Brewer, then professor of organisational behaviour at Yale University, described the consequent 'flawed decision making, self-deception, introversion and a diminished curiosity about the world outside the perfect place'. The organisational barricade became more rigid, the illusion of perfection erected another obstacle to learning and change and, fourteen years before it happened, the scene was set for the next disaster.

During the Cold War, NASA represented the fight for superiority between the USA and Russia. Money was no object but in the decade after the Cold War ended, its budget was slashed. This must have added considerable pressure to NASA, making it more likely their defences would escalate unhealthily. As circumstances change, our individual and organisational defences fluctuate in an attempt to maintain an equilibrium: they become thinner and more porous, or thicker and more rigid.

NASA exemplifies the necessity of preventing defences from solidifying. One way of doing this is to encourage new staff to speak about what they see before they become part of the organisation's defence system. New people often spot the peculiarities and, like the child who said the emperor had no clothes, can voice things established staff no longer notice or have learnt not to mention.

Most importantly, decalcifying defences requires attending to the tides of anxiety in the workplace. Looking after these and containing them emotionally, increases the likelihood of maintaining barriers and reducing barricades.

My work with the surgeons exemplified this: when I could contain their anxiety, they could resist turning their barriers into barricades. But when I couldn't contain them, or external events overwhelmed them, their barricades went up, calcified and became impenetrable.

7

Good Enough

At the age of twenty-five, Kris was the youngest team leader in the UK headquarters of an international charity. Tall and long-limbed, with olive skin, green eyes and a mop of brown curly hair, he seemed unaware of, or perhaps tried to ignore, the effect of his looks. Kris always got noticed.

Using the inheritance from his grandmother and savings ferreted away over years, he'd bought a one-bedroomed flat in Walthamstow, north-east London. He loved having his own space and spent hours redecorating and hunting down eclectic pieces of second-hand furniture. He had friends and a full social life. Kris, you felt, was on his way and would thrive in all aspects of his life.

The charity offered him coaching to help his transition into leadership. When we spoke on the phone, he told me it had taken him a while to find the right person. I felt vaguely uneasy, but his enthusiasm swept this away. When Kris twice postponed our exploratory meeting, my unease returned. At our first session, I mentioned the postponement; he blamed the pressure of work. Since it wasn't just once, I said, maybe there was more to it than that?

Bowing his head, Kris spoke softly. 'I suppose it was also

my need to have everything right and fully prepared before starting anything new.'

'You're a perfectionist?' I asked.

'I have high standards, if that's what you mean. I hate mistakes.'

'That's tough,' I said. 'Everyone makes mistakes sometimes.'

'You can avoid mistakes if you're careful.'

I told him about the psychoanalyst Donald Winnicott's phrase the 'good enough mother'. A good enough parent is devoted to their baby and also gets things wrong. They love their child, but accept that they sometimes feel angry, resentful and occasionally hateful towards the baby whose constant demands make them feel inadequate. They struggle with, yet can tolerate, their negative feelings towards their child and their child's negative feelings about them.

Kris looked sceptical yet quizzical. I carried on, explaining that rather than being a poor second to the fantasy of an unequivocally devoted parent, the 'good enough' one helps children learn about human imperfection. Without this crucial lesson, forming close relationships is always difficult.

I suggested that 'good enough' applies to all our roles, whether as parent, boss, employee, colleague, son or daughter, partner or friend.

'Sounds like an excuse for inadequacy,' Kris said.

'Inadequate isn't good enough,' I replied.

Sitting on the edge of the sofa, he told me his boss had reprimanded him for handing in a report late. 'I stayed up until 2 a.m. trying to finish it but it wasn't quite right, so I carried on the next day and then, well, then it was late. When my boss told me off, I felt terrible.'

'*Not* good enough?' I asked.

He nodded glumly. 'I couldn't face anyone so hid in the

toilet to fill the time before I could go home.' He bent to retie the laces in his sneakers.

'You feel this very keenly,' I said.

Kris nodded. 'She tries not to show it, but my boss feels really let down by me.'

'Do you know that? Perhaps you imagine she feels more let down than she does.'

'But I *have* let her down. Repeatedly. And she says I'm talented, which makes me feel worse. My behaviour is unforgivable.'

Kris had given in reports late twice before. His boss pointed out that it meant she had almost no time to draw recommendations from them for the senior team. She had to either push all her other work aside or she'd send the recommendations late. I noticed a disconnect between his boss's mild words and the major humiliation Kris felt, but suspected that mentioning this would add to his embarrassment. Instead, I commented on the pain he felt at being seen in anything less than a good light.

'I never get in trouble.'

'Does your boss ever praise you?'

'Yes, she tells me she appreciates my hard work and commitment. She says that quite often actually. And how talented I am.' He looked away.

'What sticks though is the infrequent criticism?' I asked. 'Maybe knowing she thinks you're talented makes you feel the need to be perfect even more. As though you have to be superhuman.'

'No, just keep high standards,' Kris said.

'I'm not sure it's your boss who's so critical of you. It seems it's you.'

Kris turned his head to look at the bookshelf. He muttered about imposter syndrome.

'Perhaps that's your internal critic talking,' I said. 'The voice many of us have that pops up to tell us we're not good enough.'

'I know that voice.'

He told me how he harangued himself, sometimes even for things he felt proud of. Buying his flat, for example, when so many people were homeless. He felt guilty because of his privilege. I suggested his inner saboteur also induced guilt.

At the end of the session, Kris paused. He turned towards me. 'I'm sort of relieved it's a thing and I'm not the only one who has that voice inside.' He smiled.

I recalled the loudness of my own internal critic before I had psychoanalysis. Freud called this part of us the 'superego'. It includes our conscience. For some of us the superego is like an internal mentor – mostly benign and just occasionally highly critical of us. It might, for instance, get us to give up smoking or resist those extra chocolates or glasses of wine. It helps us to notice when we're about to react in unreasonable ways or cause harm to ourselves or other people.

For some though, like Kris, and me pre-analysis, the superego is harsh and constantly critical. The psychoanalyst Mike Brearley, who first consulted to me about the seminar series I ran on leadership and psychoanalysis, and continued to think with me about this book, described it like a 'dictator or hanging judge'. Before analysis, this part of me took any opportunity to persecute me. If I didn't get promoted, for instance, or fell out with a friend, or a relationship ended, it taunted me. No wonder, it said, who were you kidding? It drummed into me – mostly unconsciously – that I wasn't good enough.

Thankfully, my superego changed during my psychoanalysis. It still berates me occasionally, but nothing like before. The easing up of this part of myself has made an enormous difference to my life and given me immeasurable relief. It allows me to strive for more, as I no longer fear its barrage of attack if I don't succeed.

At our next session, Kris told me his history. His father had come with his family to England from Greece in 1971. Dad was six and his parents had fled from the right-wing junta. Kris remembered moments of fear and horror but mostly Dad's stories recounted happy memories and his acute longing for his country of birth. He met Kris's Welsh mother at work. They were both senior civil servants: Dad in the Foreign Office and Mum in the Treasury.

Kris described his parents as liberal. They didn't enforce bedtimes or homework and there were few rules. When he was seventeen, his girlfriend came to visit for a weekend during the summer holiday. His friends had to sneak their girlfriends in and out of their bedrooms, but Kris's father gave him a packet of condoms and his parents let his girlfriend share his bed.

'We didn't actually have sex,' he told me. 'Just heavy petting.'

After his A levels, Kris followed in his mother's footsteps and went to Oxford University to study history. He travelled in Africa for a few months before joining the charity he still worked for as a junior researcher.

'I was always in the top stream at school and Mum and Dad expected nothing less than top grades. They never even considered that I may not go to university or do really well. Luckily, I got an upper second. They were fine with that. I wasn't. I'd been on course for a first.'

The 'failure' of an upper second-class degree felt irrecoverable to him. The pain still smarted. He had repetitive, anxious dreams about being late for one of his final exams or being back at university with a second chance but mucking it up again.

The following session we focused on his leadership. Kris's instincts were good. He appreciated and supported his staff and gave them regular feedback. Sometimes these positive instincts got lost though and he overreacted, coming down sharply on staff when he considered them 'sloppy'. I wondered if the perfectionism he expected from himself extended to his staff, and whether he was as unable to forgive them as he was himself. If so, they'd soon feel persecuted by him. I waited for the right time to say this, concerned that he'd use it against himself rather than as an insight for development.

Lateness soon got Kris into trouble again. This time, having worked into the early hours of the morning to get a report 'just right', he'd overslept and arrived late to a rare presentation to all the staff by the chief executive.

'I tried to come in unnoticed, but my boss saw me and looked daggers at me. She told me afterwards that I'd made us both look bad.'

'Do you think on some level you wanted to get into trouble?' I asked, thinking he'd unconsciously provoked his boss into telling him off.

'No. Why would I want that? I hate it. I feel so humiliated.'

'Perhaps the "not good enough" voice likes it?' I asked.

'Maybe,' he said and changed the subject, talking about superficial issues for the short time remaining.

I sat in the dim light of dusk after Kris left, his story replaying in my mind. Unlike some clients whose critical parents had contributed to instilling a critical superego in their unconscious, Kris's harsh superego seemed to be a response to his parents' lack of boundaries and authority. I remembered reading about adolescents typically searching for a strong authority figure to keep them in check while also caring for them. Kris's superego didn't do the caring and overdid the checking; perhaps its harshness compensated for the insecurity caused by his parents' lack of rules.

Kris cancelled the next two sessions, due again, he said, to the pressure of work. I suspected he'd turned back to his usual postponement because I'd pushed the idea of the internal critic too far. When he came again, he was fifteen minutes late. He sat down hurriedly and told me he'd been rejected for a job in a children's charity.

'They were right,' he said, 'Of course they didn't give me the job.'

'Because you don't have the experience?'

'Because I'm not good enough.'

'The words of your inner critic,' I said.

I asked him why he hadn't mentioned the application to me and used coaching to think it through. Kris seemed surprised. He said he ought to be able to sort these things out for himself. I didn't pursue that for the moment, but asked why he'd applied for the job when he loved his current one.

'I should be progressing.'

A harsh inner critic, I told him, is full of 'should' and 'ought'. 'And isn't applying for a job you won't get more like self-sabotage than progress?'

I heard the crowd of 'shoulds' and 'oughts' that used to plague me. Did Kris need therapy rather than coaching?

A job came up a short while later in his own organisation. Unlike with the children's charity, he had the right experience and qualifications and his boss encouraged him to apply. But he didn't because the humiliation of not getting it would be unbearable. He regretted his decision when the successful candidate was announced.

'I'm much better than him. Now he's ahead and he's younger than me.' I sensed superiority behind his resentment.

'You think you're better than him, but you couldn't risk applying,' I said.

'That inside voice?'

I nodded.

'It does hold me back doesn't it?' he asked.

I agreed and mentioned therapy. He said he'd started to think about that too.

A bird sang close by. Kris gestured towards the window. 'I don't suppose they have a second horrible voice playing in their head.'

The next month, Kris told me he'd started going out with a woman he'd previously rejected. Now, he'd decided to give her a chance. We acknowledged that this was probably a result of his internal critic's judgement easing a little.

'I actually really like her.' He smiled shyly.

Coaching was helping Kris be a little less hard on himself, but by now I was sure that only therapy could modify this part of him. I'd been wrong about Kris being on his way when I first met him. His internal critic and impossible perfectionism held him back.

I imagined how the previous months would have unfolded if Kris's superego had been benign rather than berating. Instead of setting him up and then, like a cruel judge, delighting in punishing him with guilt and shame, it would have supported him by warning him he was about to let his perfectionism get in his way, reminding him to go to bed on time and stopping him oversleeping. It would have prompted him to get help instead of rushing off the wrong job application and encouraged him to apply for the right one.

A few weeks later, he told me he'd decided not to pursue therapy as things were going well. I suggested he could come back to it if he wanted and repeated my offer to get recommendations of therapists. I hoped he'd find his way to this before too long. He was young and, if he had therapy now, instead of enduring the pain his internal critic caused him and needlessly expending energy to appease or ignore it, he could cultivate a supportive internal presence that could help him fulfil his potential and create the life he wanted.

I never found out whether or not Kris decided to go into therapy as he postponed and cancelled sessions, until he simply drifted away from coaching. Perhaps he found our work intolerable because it provoked too much pain and shame. Or perhaps he knew at some level that it would bring him face to face with the possibility that his authoritarian internal judge was in part a reaction to his parents.

Or maybe he thought I wasn't good enough.

8

Paranoia

Fearing he was about to lose his job, David came to see me for a consultation. He was head of the private clients department in a law firm and wanted help in thinking about whether to quit before he was pushed.

A tall, suave man in a well-tailored suit, David had been with the firm since its inception, ten years earlier, and had worked closely with James, the founder and managing partner. They'd started with private clients, handling family law (divorce, custody, child support, domestic violence), personal injury, medical negligence, wills, tax and probate. Three years ago, the firm had set up the second department, involving business law (consumer contracts, supply chains, licensing, franchising, intellectual property), corporation tax, as well as incorporation of companies, mergers and acquisitions.

Everything had changed since then. Logan, the head of commercial and corporate law, wanted shot of the private clients department because of its low revenue. The commercial lawyers brought in substantially more money but, David explained, they could bill aggressively, whereas in private law, in which individuals rather than companies foot the bill, that wasn't possible.

David described Logan as exacting and driven. 'He's at the

office for twelve or fourteen hours each day and disdainful of the private client lawyers who work more normal hours.'

Not because they're lazy, as Logan infers, he said, but because private clients work doesn't involve the huge spikes of activity that goes with commercial law during, for example, a merger or acquisition. I asked if the ways of working in the two strands of law clashed.

'No, it's Logan. He's ruthless. All the commercial lawyers are. They see private clients work as pedestrian, not the cut and thrust of commercial law. That's all about money, mergers, profit. For us it's about people, families, the welfare of children.'

'So there's a clash of values?'

'Yes, in a way.'

I wondered if there were any positive reasons for him leaving, but David insisted there weren't – this was purely about going before he was pushed.

'Logan's like a bird of prey, always swooping about.' He constantly accused the private client lawyers of not doing enough billable hours and not recording their time properly which meant they undercharged.

'He sees us as frivolous. Last week he was furious because one of my team brought cakes and drinks and invited everyone to mark his fiftieth birthday. The do was at 5.30. Logan complained afterwards that 5.30 is part of the working day, not time for drinking. Ridiculous. Sometimes if he sees me reading the newspaper over a sandwich at lunchtime, he tuts loudly.'

Logan sounded unpleasant, perhaps ruthless and certainly persecutory, but that didn't necessarily mean he wanted rid of David. Why was David so sure of this?

'It's obvious. Start with me, as head of private clients and then it's a short step to scrapping the whole department.'

'That's what the managing partner wants?'

'Of course.'

'Why?'

'Because it's best for the firm financially.'

'Has something been said to make you so certain of his intention?'

'No, but it's obvious.'

'Not to me.'

David sighed heavily. He stared at the fireplace before muttering that I didn't get it. It seemed there was no space in his mind for anything other than his interpretation of events. I agreed with him that I didn't understand.

He held his head in his hands almost as though he was trying to hold the pieces of his mind together. After a moment, he tried again.

'Partnership meetings used to be convivial, but now it's all about who's brought in the most fees and got more new clients. It's all pressure and blame.'

'I understand the change must be stressful and painful, but I'm still not clear why it means you're about to lose your job.'

'But . . .' He stopped.

His tone softer, David explained that he'd been made redundant when his previous firm cut back during the 2008 financial crisis. He hadn't spotted the signs at the time. He wasn't going to let that happen again. It made sense of my emerging hypothesis: in his paranoid state of mind, David's beliefs and assumptions had become facts. Perhaps, back in 2008, David was gullible, with an insufficient sense of persecution and paranoia, so it had gone into overdrive now.

I thought of a friend who'd rung me a few days ago. She'd given a paper at a conference. Her boss had told her he'd attend but hadn't. Though disappointed, my friend didn't worry, but when he made no mention of her paper at lunchtime, she thought she must have offended him. Perhaps not attending or saying anything was payback for the time she didn't go to his paper. No, she'd asked him beforehand if he'd mind so it couldn't be that. But then again it could be payback anyway. What if he was cutting her out? What had she done? On she went, articulating the dialogue that filled her mind with the noise of low-level paranoia. Its drone often whirrs unnoticed in us and in our organisations.

It happens moment to moment out of work, too. When, for instance, you're convinced a neighbour deliberately swapped your new dustbin for a grotty old one, while on another day, in a different state of mind, you'd know the binmen put the bins back in the wrong place.

The psychoanalyst Melanie Klein identified two fundamental mental positions: in one, we split people and things into 'good' and 'bad' and experience ourselves, others and the world simplistically. In the other, we manage more complexity, and consequently are more in touch with reality.

We begin life in the split, black and white state. Our brains are not yet fully formed and can't manage complexity. In this place, we coo in pleasure at our parents who are there whenever we want or need them, and contort in rage if they're in the toilet when we want to feed or they answer the phone when we need a cuddle. Klein said that because we're unable to manage the complexity of our intensely contrasting feelings, in our minds we divide the parent in two: the 'good' one and the 'bad' one.

All being well, babies move to a more integrated position at around six months old and start to comprehend that the good and bad parent are the same person. But the splitting and polarisation don't go away. As we grow up, we develop adult versions of these two states of mind and move back and forth between them throughout life. We often return to the split position during times of stress.

President George W. Bush's declaration in 2001 after the attack on the twin towers exemplified it: 'You're either with us or against us . . .' His 'axis of evil' implied that 'we' were good and only good, and 'they' were bad and only bad.

George W. Bush isn't the only politician to use this part of our mind to whip up our paranoia; it's a common weapon. Others, we're told – foreigners, refugees, the EU – will take our jobs and our housing. Racism thrives on this mental state. Wars depend on it.

The split and paranoid position crops up regularly in the workplace: an 'us and them' divide, emphatic views about who's right and wrong, and the imagined machinations when staff become convinced that every communication or change is malign.

If this was where David was coming from, I needed to help him shift into the more integrated, reality-based position. To get a clearer picture, I asked him about his client work. As he outlined some of the cases he dealt with, I imagined the division of furniture, photos, friends, sometimes even children, when a marriage breaks up. The intransigence and distrust of some divorcing couples, fighting over custody or to get the best financial settlement. I saw how paranoia and persecution could infect their clients and easily transfer to the lawyers.

But I was still unsure how much truth, if any, lay behind David's conviction that the firm no longer wanted him. I asked about the managing partner's view of the private clients department. David said he was a family lawyer so had a soft spot for their department but relied on Logan as the rainmaker. The money he and his colleagues in commercial and corporate clients brought in gave them greater standing than the private client lawyers. But no, he admitted when I asked, he hadn't talked to the managing partner about the future of private clients. And no, he hadn't talked to Logan either.

'You're not convinced I've got this right, are you?'

'Not really. Are you?'

'It's possible I haven't.' I was relieved: David's mind was shifting.

He continued, 'We built the firm on private clients – it's part of our reputation. Sometimes private clients bring their firms to us and become commercial ones and vice versa.'

'So there are advantages to having both departments?'

'I suppose so.'

I asked why he was so sure that Logan, though exacting and hard to work with, was malicious.

'I suppose I'm seeing ill intent in everything aren't I?'

This acknowledgement marked the shift from one mental position to the other. The persecution had receded, and David could stand back and reflect on himself rather than being stuck in the grip of paranoia.

We talked about the tension between the two departments representing the intractable stance between adversarial parties and the persecutory paranoid feelings legal battles evoke. How the absolutes of the law, with its black and white rights and wrongs, compliance and infringements, encouraged paranoia.

'I haven't always made it easy for Logan. I jump on everything he says, swiping before he does.'

'Because you assume ill intent?'

'Yes. Now, I'm less certain.'

The certainty of the split and paranoid position is key to its attraction. In contrast, the more integrated position involves dealing with nuance as well as facing ourselves and taking responsibility for our behaviour.

Looking more relaxed, David told me that he and his wife were going through a nightmare house move. They thought they'd sold their place, but their buyer kept them hanging on and then dropped out at the last minute. And, to top it off, they were gazumped on the house they'd fallen in love with. Now they were at square one again.

'No wonder you became more paranoid at work and desperate for certainty, even if the certainty was bad,' I said.

We were nearing the end of our session. We discussed what David would do. He decided to talk to Logan and probably to the managing partner, too.

A fortnight later, David emailed me to say he was staying at the firm. The conversation with Logan had been hard but helpful. Logan, it turned out, thought David wanted rid of him too. They still didn't like each other but David thought they'd be more able to work together and check things out before their assumptions took hold.

David had shifted his state of mind in a couple of hours. Sometimes we take minutes, days or months. A few people never leave the split, paranoid place. It's not that one position is good and the other bad: the paranoid position can bring energy and commitment. It's only problematic if we stay there too long and too rigidly.

For most of us, the movement between these two fundamental positions is an ongoing process. Not only is this unavoidable, but the cycle is necessary for our development. We need to recognise though that like the mechanism of projection and the different metaphorical glasses we wear, our interpretation of people and events changes according to our mental position.

and then dropped out at the last minute. [illegible] they were unattached so the money they'd taken in [illegible] they were at [illegible]

[illegible] wonder you became more passionate at work and [illegible] for certainty [illegible] I said.

[illegible] He decided to [illegible] open and [illegible] the [illegible] parents.

[illegible]

[illegible] and [illegible] of [illegible] people [illegible] and the other [illegible] and [illegible]

[illegible] and the different [illegible] of people [illegible]

9

Belonging

We sat in groups of four, our small desks arranged to form a square. The other three girls chattered to me eagerly. Recognising the rising intonation at the end of their sentences, I smiled tentatively as I couldn't answer the questions. By mid-morning, I couldn't manage the smiles either; I bit my lip to stop the tears. By lunchtime, the other children had given up trying to include me.

I was five years old and this was my first day at school. We'd moved to Dundee from Harlow in Essex the week before and I found the Dundonian dialect incomprehensible. The reception class was full, so I'd joined the year above. The other children all knew each other and understood this strange place called school. Not being able to speak with them left me alone and excluded.

My family had only been in the UK for four years, so my parents were not yet accustomed to it. Dundee, on the north bank of the River Tay, with its shipping industry, mills and rain, was especially strange. To my mother, who yearned for the light and blazing sunshine of Israel where she'd grown up, it seemed perpetually underlit. The grey brick of the buildings, dull and dirty with age, matched the weather. Grey imbued our school, the blocks of flats in the three-sided square we lived in and the back-to-back slum houses covering swathes of the city, laundry billowing from the pulleys stretched across their upper-floor windows.

My parents, sister and I immigrated to the UK from Israel when I was fifteen months old. We spent a year in Bristol, where Dad's family had already settled and he'd got a lectureship post, before three years in Harlow and then Dundee. With my parents' strong foreign accents and customs, I must have already sensed that we were outsiders, but starting school in Dundee was my first conscious experience of the visceral pain of not belonging.

I know from my clients this pain occurs daily in the workplace. For some, the organisational culture is familiar, while for others, the subtle norms are totally foreign. 'We don't do it like that round here,' people say to newcomers, putting them in their place, reminding them that to fit in they need to learn not just the local accent, but a new language.

Like the 'different' person in the workplace, who has to twist and turn to belong, or deal with the consequences of not doing so, my family had to manage the pride and pain of difference. We ate different food and had different customs. We celebrated Christmas and Easter differently and my parents spoke to each other in another language. No one knew how to pronounce our surname. Nor, at that time, the first names of myself and my sister.

My parents had deep roots, but not to the country we lived in. As refugees, not belonging was etched into their identities. They'd experienced extreme trauma as children, fleeing their countries of origin – my mother from Germany, my father from Czechoslovakia – where a number of their relatives died. They went to Palestine where the low-level fighting that began in 1947 escalated into the first Arab–Israeli War in 1948, when the British Mandate ended and the Israeli Declaration of Independence was announced.

In the UK, we didn't belong to a community of people from our own country or with our background. Living here, Mum inferred, was a transitory misadventure. It lasted the rest of her life. She spent years longing to return home. The weather depressed her. She found the temperament bewildering and alienating. She hated the flavourless, overcooked food. 'They don't use garlic,' she'd exclaim incredulously. 'They've never heard of aubergines.'

While belonging often eluded us, my sister and I excelled in adaptability. We had to. After a few months I spoke Dundonian with a perfect local accent, had friends and fitted in. The following August, when the new school year began, I went to the large tree in the small playground where my friends and I always met. I stood alone under the branches. Having moved from the infants to the junior school, my friends had gone to the big playground nearby. Despite coming fifth out of the thirty children in the class, and my parents' protestations, the school insisted I stay back so I'd be in the right year for my age. As my friends beckoned and called to me, I shook my head. I felt ashamed and forlorn. My hard won belonging evaporated like steam, as though it had never existed. I did no better academically than I had the year before.

After two years in Dundee, my father got a senior lectureship at one of the London University colleges and we headed back across the border, to Letchworth in Hertfordshire. The Quakers owned the land of this garden city: it had wide tree-lined pavements, a garden for every house and strict planning rules that included a ban on selling alcohol in public places.

The contrast between Dundee and Letchworth strained our adaptability. From the only school in Dundee that, at the time, didn't cane girls, we went to a private progressive Quaker school in Letchworth. It was my mother's choice; my parents separated while we were in Dundee and, fearing their marriage wouldn't last, she wanted us to be able to board if necessary.

In the Quaker school, our foreignness didn't matter – plenty of children came from abroad. Boarder versus day pupil did though; we were day pupils while the majority boarded. Money also mattered. At the age of seven, I knew we were poor, but not as poor as Yvonne, the poorest in my class. I held tight to that one rung of difference. The emphasis on creativity and music suited me. I wrote stories, learnt the clarinet and made friends. I belonged once again.

Attached to school, my friends, the town and my clarinet teacher, I didn't want to leave Letchworth. But my father got a chair at Aston University in Birmingham and we moved once more. I joined the fourth year of the local junior school. My Dundonian, which had turned to the flat tones and accentuated vowels of Hertfordshire, now morphed to the nasal twang of Brummie. Quickly acquiring accents had become part of my way of fitting in.

Despite my best efforts to integrate, my difference often showed. Shortly after I started my new school, we had to bring money for the Parent Teacher Association. With no idea of the usual amount and no one to ask, my parents gave me five pounds. I watched in rising panic as the other children handed in 50p or £1. Just before my turn, I put the five-pound note in my desk and gave £1 from my pocket money. During assembly the teacher went through our desks and came across the five-pound note. I was hauled out of the hall and sent to the headmaster accused of stealing.

The five-pound note pronounced our class. Most children at this junior school were from the local council estate. We lived on the opposite side of the school, on a wide street with large, detached houses, each distinct and set back from the road, behind spacious front gardens and driveways. I'd leapt from the second poorest in the class in Letchworth, to an entirely new status in Birmingham – one I found extremely uncomfortable.

My parents had bought what they thought fitted our new station. Our 'professorial' house had a wood-panelled square hall as big as many people's living rooms, a breakfast room as well as kitchen, living room and dining room where the table stood lost in the centre of the large space. A wide staircase led to four bedrooms. The fact that the house was a wreck – a 'doer upper' – didn't change its stature. I hated the message it sent about our wealth and class.

When I went for tea with a school friend on the council estate, her mum asked me what my dad did. I told her he worked at the university. 'A cleaner?' 'Yes,' I said, the betrayal sticking like bile in my mouth with an aftertaste of guilt. Admitting the truth seemed impossible since it meant revealing the extent of our difference and privilege.

We rarely talk about class, yet it remains pervasive in British society and its organisations and is one of the unspoken components of belonging. The leader of a team I coached in an elite university came from a working-class family in the north-west. Her dad had been a coal miner. She told me about her pride and amazement in ending up where she was, but also her fear of being pushed out or getting things wrong because she couldn't read the unspoken code that everyone else understood.

A few months into my new school in Birmingham, I took the eleven-plus. At the Quaker school, we measured tennis courts instead of learning our times tables and wrote stories rather than learning how to form sentences. I passed, but not well enough to join my sister at the grammar school. I went to a terrifyingly huge comprehensive with eleven streams per year. For years I dreamt about getting lost in its endless corridors.

On the first day, we gathered for English. One by one, we stood in front of the class at the teacher's desk as he registered us. 'You've misspelt your name,' he told me. I had a stock answer, used to people correcting the spelling of my surname, but he was talking about my shortened first name.

'There are two 'bs' in Gabby', he said. I explained that it came from Gabriella, which only has one 'b'.

'Well, in that case,' he boomed across the room, 'the "a" is like in "stable" not "apple". And *Gaby*' – he emphasised and extended the a – 'means IDIOT in Old English.'

He stroked his beard, smirking. In the raucous laughter from my classmates, an unstoppable blush sped across my neck and face.

The teacher's humiliating words emphasised my foreignness, my not belonging. Making friends changed this. I instinctively sought out similarity and became best friends with two middle-class girls from among the mostly working-class children. My friends' fathers were academics like mine. Known as the 'terrible three', we became inseparable.

My mother was right; their marriage fell apart a few months after we got to Birmingham and they divorced during my first year at secondary school. Long before I knew the word, I experienced the effect of stigma. I felt it when my parents separated in Dundee and, most acutely, when they divorced in Birmingham. Although commonplace now, at the time I didn't know anyone else whose parents had split up. The stigma of being the girl from a 'broken home' formed another obstacle between me and belonging. The teachers watched my every move, nodding sagely when my behaviour deteriorated, as though I was an example in a book.

My sister and I didn't have the security of a nationality

passed down the generations, or of growing up in one place. We didn't have a network of relatives, or adults you call 'aunty' because you've known them all your lives. We weren't part of a religious community or clubs. But I belonged with my friends and held on fiercely to that.

At university in Lancaster ways of belonging broadened: as well as with friends, I belonged in my college, with fellow students in my subject and the university as a whole. This protective layer around me affected my identity. At school I'd tried to dumb down as a way of fitting in, but at university learning became joyful, and I no longer tried to hide my ability.

My sense of belonging and identity continued to expand in the world of work. In my first permanent post at a further education college, I quickly felt part of a community with a shared purpose. I found colleagues as passionate about what we did as I was. I belonged to my team, department, the union and the college. Belonging provided camaraderie, fun and security. With the attachment it offered I, like many of my colleagues, worked far harder than was required. I was loyal and automatically advocated for the college. The benefits of belonging – for me and for my workplace – continued in my next jobs.

They remained intact when I first worked for a national company but when we relocated from central London to the Midlands and I was promoted to head of department, belonging evaporated and work became miserable. With no training and only the experience of leading a small team in a local organisation, I ran a large department. At the same time as relocating, the company introduced a major restructuring. They mismanaged these changes spectacularly.

We moved from a beautiful, elegant, buzzy part of central London, near galleries, shops, restaurants and a large peaceful park, to a nondescript industrial town. Since the company only offered a relocation package to a handful of us, 90 per cent of staff left.

I worked harder and harder, but my 'to do' list never diminished. I'd get up in the dark, drive past the local prison in a state of stomach-churning anxiety and arrive at 7.30 at the new, open-plan office on a forsaken building site. The company occupied one of the first buildings in a soulless business park on the outskirts of the soulless town, its large glossy sign incongruous with the mud and the cranes. I'd walk down a deserted corridor to my glass fishbowl office.

With practically no breaks, I'd leave twelve hours later when desks, corridors and the derelict, windy car park had emptied once again. I went home accompanied by my ever-present clutching anxiety. Darkness and cold and the small relief of getting through another day, quickly undone by the prospect of the days to follow, marked my way home.

As chaos grew, splintered relationships, cliques and exclusion spread. The other two heads of department were good friends and had worked for the company for decades. We fell out. Isolated and beleaguered, I worked in the evenings and at weekends. The external pressure mixed with the pressure in my mind. I felt culpable and a failure.

Belonging, like our defences, shields us. It provides a degree of both psychological and physical immunity against the struggle of being human. It fulfils our need to be part of a group and takes away the pain of exclusion. Without it, the misery and stress at work became unbearable. I resigned.

Years later, I thought I'd found a much longed for professional home. Shortly after I joined the organisation, the scope of our work, which I'd been so excited by, changed and then spun in flux. Initially, I took every new direction presented emphatically by my boss at face value. My colleagues and I became ever more discombobulated as we tried to keep up with the constantly moving remit and goalposts. One minute we were definitely going to merge with another organisation, the next we would certainly remain as we were, the next we would move premises. We were in free-fall and my colleagues left in droves.

The few of us remaining took on more and more work. We did in fact move. It proved to be the last straw for me. We went from the organisation's main building, where I felt nurtured and supported by many interesting colleagues from other departments, to a scruffy, desolate building on our own. I hated it there. I felt cut off and lonely; isolated once again, like I had as a child in Dundee.

My dream of a professional home ebbed away as I understood that in this organisation I would always look in from the outside. Belonging was reserved for old-timers and those who submitted to the self-idealising organisational culture. As all my energy went into surviving both the workload and painful emotional experience, my performance and creativity decreased. I knew I could fight my way closer to fitting in by submerging myself to the culture, but I wasn't prepared to. I decided, as I had years before, to resign.

My experience of being on the border – of places, schools and organisations – and my sensitivity to difference and exclusion provided an invaluable grounding for my work as a consultant, where you're always on the boundary, always adapting to new clients and their organisational cultures. Instead of belonging professionally to a single institution, I belong through my professional relationships, affiliations and community.

Belonging can surprise me. As, for instance, the only foreign member of staff in an experiential workshop in India, I thought I'd finally feel English or British. Instead, I felt white.

On the other hand, in the aftermath of the 2005 London bombs, I discovered I felt like a Londoner.

For me, belonging is a feeling that slips and slides; sometimes it encircles me, at other times it moves away like a receding tide. The ever-shifting currents of the workplace emphasise its unpredictable nature. Yet, however elusive and uncertain its substance, like most people, I find belonging profoundly affects my state of mind and ability to be at my best.

PART TWO
LOSING OURSELVES

10

Losing the Plot

The phone calls started before I'd finished breakfast. Jayesh, the communications director, was the first to tell me that the chief executive, Tim, had just emailed from New York. He'd resigned. He'd only been with them for four months and now, with no warning, no notice, he'd gone back to the US. Until a week ago, no one but Eleanor, the chair, knew that his wife had already returned home.

I'd consulted to the company a few years before. Eleanor had rung me two months ago and asked me to facilitate a workshop for the board and senior leadership team as they were going through significant change. The workshop was supposed to take place the following day.

Within a couple of weeks of joining, Tim, with the board's approval, had introduced a major programme of restructuring and reorganising work processes. Ten days ago, they'd begun a consultation process with staff about the proposed new structure.

Before I could think about the implications of Tim's leaving, the phone went again. I could barely make out the vice-chair Amber's torrent of words.

'New York—Why?—Bloody mess—' Her words slowed. 'We put 50 per cent of jobs at risk for God's sake. I couldn't understand why Tim was so keen to begin the consultation when the plan for the restructure and reorganisation was nowhere near ready. Now I get it. He knew he was leaving, deserting us. It's unbelievable. I feel so let down.'

Tim kept telling them the consultation needed to go ahead quickly so that the period of uncertainty for staff was as short as possible. He'd argued that no plan is perfect before consultation; the whole point is to get feedback and finalise it afterwards.

'Bullshit,' Amber snorted down the phone. 'He just wanted to get it done as fast as possible so he could go. And he didn't even wait for it to be done.'

She suspected Eleanor had known Tim was going but failed to warn them. She and Tim were 'joined at the hip', and Eleanor had also pushed for the consultation to go ahead, so she must have been in on his sudden departure. But surely Eleanor couldn't have gone along with this?

'I don't know what to think or do.' Amber, usually so solid and composed, sounded distraught.

I gulped down a glass of water. The phone went again. Nigel, the finance director, told me one of the senior team and three other staff had left last week. None of them had jobs to go to. Three grievance procedures had also been taken against the company.

'Eleanor's in a complete state. Losing her temper, yelling at people, blaming the senior team for everything. She's talking about resigning. Maybe that's best. Or it might be the last straw and break us.'

Kate, the director of human resources, rang towards the end of the afternoon. Her voice shook as she said she hadn't agreed with the way the restructuring was being done and was horrified by the speed of the consultation yet hadn't been able to stand up to Tim or Eleanor. 'I feel terrible about that.

So weak. But I can't afford to lose my job.' The letter to staff about the consultation went out in her name and she was now at the receiving end of their hostility. I wondered if she'd leave, too, even without a job to go to.

In the evening Eleanor rang. We talked about the workshop; she agreed that I would enable difficult conversations and she'd try not to get defensive. She sounded calm and thoughtful, yet from what people had told me, her moods went up and down from moment to moment. I didn't know what had caused her to lose her way with the consultation and with Tim. I liked her and wanted to protect her, but I knew I couldn't. My task was to help the company, even if that meant Eleanor resigned or was asked to step down; even if she lost it in the workshop.

I'd come off the phone spinning. Jayesh, stunned; Kate so distressed and obviously bullied by Tim; Amber and Nigel, who normally kept their heads and made sound decisions, both lost. I tried to order my mind. Why had Tim left so abruptly? Perhaps his wife gave him an ultimatum. Or, even if she hadn't, perhaps the strain on his marriage had been too much. Prioritising their marriage over his job was admirable but squeezing the restructuring to fit his wish to return home and then leaving without a word was unprofessional and unethical. Had he lost the plot? Had the board and the senior team?

My breath was white in the early morning fog as I walked to the tube the next day. Exiting in central London, I enjoyed the rare quiet of the streets. The café I frequented when I went to the company was just opening, the staff busy putting out pastries, granola bowls, shakes and sandwiches. I sat at a window table and looked at the programme I'd hastily redesigned last night. My schedule allowed time to discuss how everyone was feeling at the outset of the workshop, what they hoped for, what they feared and how we wanted to work together.

The café filled up with people on their way to work, some having breakfast meetings, a couple poring over a well-thumbed guidebook. I finished my second espresso and left. The fog hung in a thin film over the now crowded streets.

The air changed as I opened the heavy double doors into the company's office; the damp dimness outside was replaced by the warmth and discreet lighting of the elegant reception area. A tiled corridor opened out into the modern extension at the back of the Victorian building. In the light and airy meeting room two clocks, one at either end of the room, showed different times. People drifted in, chatting to each other in subdued voices around the table laid out with coffee and biscuits. Eleanor's imposing figure crossed the room towards me. Her hair, greyer than when I'd last seen her, was in the same old-fashioned bun. William, one of the long-standing board members, joined us, coffee in one hand, overcoat in the other. Jayesh came over and took his coat for him. William had mentored Jayesh when he started with the company. They nodded at each other affectionately.

We sat in the large circle of chairs. The senior leadership team – Kate, Jayesh, and Nigel – were side by side. One chair remained empty. Who was missing? Nigel, who'd set up the room, counted: seventeen chairs. He recounted, this time walking around the circle, his perfectly polished black shoes gleaming against the pale blue carpet. Seventeen. Shaking his head, he pulled the empty chair out of the circle. 'Seventeen includes Tim,' he said.

They sat as though bracing themselves for what was to come. To get the most out of the workshop, they needed to be honest, they agreed. To listen to each other, not make assumptions, not blame. And they needed courage, including the courage to speak up.

We explored how they'd arrived at this point. They talked about the rush to implement the restructure, with no time to properly discuss anything. Decisions made on the hop, a 'rubbish' business case for the reorganisation: no details, figures done on the back of an envelope. They were totally unready to consult with staff about the proposed structure, but . . . the voices tailed off. Eleanor sat motionless, ignoring the glances directed at her.

'But?' I asked.

'Somehow,' Jayesh said, 'against our better judgement we went ahead.'

My stomach contracted; their account confirmed my suspicions from yesterday's phone calls. They'd splintered, lost the plot. An image of my psychoanalyst appeared in my mind. Facing my insane parts during my analysis had been hell, but ultimately so helpful.

I'd believed you were either mad or not, so if I was mad, I must have always been mad and always would be. I was immensely relieved to discover that – however sane we are – we all have insane parts and insane moments. Sanity and insanity, I learnt, are generally far from fixed; we lose our minds and can recover them again.

I wondered how far into insanity the board and senior team had drifted. Could the company collapse? There wasn't time to skirt around so, supported by my internalised analyst, I told them they'd lost their minds.

'Psychosis means losing touch with reality. That's what you did.'

They stared at me.

William sat forward. 'But the plan might have worked if Tim hadn't bloody left.' Others agreed eagerly.

'It's hard to credit his behaviour,' I said. 'But you all went ahead with the consultation, you put 50 per cent of jobs at risk, even though you knew the plan was full of holes. You let the whole restructure and reorganisation depend on one person. You're deluding yourselves to think it would have worked if Tim had stayed.'

Amber broke the silence that followed my words. 'We haven't talked about who knew what when.' Furtive looks passed between them, people crossed legs, ankles, arms. Eleanor, rotating her wedding ring round and round her finger, pursed her lips.

'Tim told me about his plan to go back to the US three months ago,' she admitted.

'That was only a month after he started,' Jayesh sounded stunned.

'Yes. I encouraged him to tell you all, but he wanted to wait. It was his news. I couldn't break confidentiality. He reassured me there was plenty of time to sort out the consultation before he went. The organisation is bigger than the chief executive. We couldn't change our plans because Tim was leaving.'

'I'm not sure this was something to keep confidential,' Jayesh said.

'I agree,' Amber said. 'Sorry, Eleanor, but didn't we need to know given the restructure? We shouldn't have let everything depend on him.'

I saw, felt, Amber's strain at opposing Eleanor; as chair and vice-chair, they worked closely together.

We heard the lunch trolley coming up the corridor, the smell of pakoras and samosas wafting into the room. I got some food and found a vacant meeting space. My thoughts turned to other teams I'd worked with who'd gone mad. Not as badly as in this case, but they too had lost the plot. The team that had a brief moment of acute insanity in a reflective session I ran fortnightly. One member commuted from Italy and always left ten minutes early to get his flight. When the group told him how infuriating and disruptive this was, he accused them of envying him for living in Rome. A woman refuted this; she didn't even like Rome. The group rallied around, all keen to disparage Rome. Twenty minutes later the woman remembered she'd never been to Rome and the group saw its craziness.

As individuals go in and out of sanity, so do teams. The psychoanalyst Wilfred Bion said that under stress they often go into what he called 'basic assumptions': unconsciously they lose sight of their real task and behave according to the diktat of the assumption that's taken them over. Bion identified three basic assumptions: 'dependence', 'fight/flight' and 'pairing'.

The board and senior team had slipped into the third of these, unconsciously setting up Eleanor and Tim as a pair to magically save them all and bring about instant transformational change without struggle or argument. Pairing has an excited edge yet is doomed because it's always future focused; the pair, whether two people or an individual with an initiative, will solve everything at some point ahead. The Messiah is coming but never arrives. Eleanor and Tim fitted this wish perfectly: she at the end of her career, driven to make her mark before retiring and he near the beginning, determined to make his mark so he could quickly move on to become chief executive of a larger organisation.

Stopping the disastrous consultation process yesterday signalled a return to sanity. Yet their eagerness to believe the plan could have worked if only Tim had stayed showed its fragility. I needed to help them consolidate the return from their disturbed state of mind.

We explored the key moments and feelings that had led

them to this place. The years of frustration built up by the previous chief executive's resistance to change, with arguments about every development, large or small: changing an operating process or the type and length of papers that went to the board. The relief they all felt when he resigned. Their excitement about the sweeping change, the complete transformation Tim offered. The promise they saw in his youthful energy, his vigorous and determined enthusiasm.

'It felt so good, a kind of renewal, when we came up with ideas about the restructure and reorganisation,' Kate said.

'It's hard to admit, but I thought we'd finally do something outstanding as a company,' Eleanor said. 'I was thrilled. I'd wanted that so much, waited so long. This was my last chance.'

'It was exciting and bonding,' another board member acknowledged. 'For the first time we were all on the same page and effecting change. It only lasted briefly, but it felt really good.'

The newest and youngest board member, Zainab, commented on the togetherness which had given her a sense of belonging.

Hesitantly, Kate, Jayesh, and Nigel described their growing doubt about Tim and the restructure and reorganisation. It started when he insisted on a ridiculously short timescale to detail every aspect of the project. He asked for their suggestions but dismissed whatever they came up with if it didn't suit his plan. There were numerous problems with the plan, yet suddenly he claimed the details didn't matter. They'd consult the staff and begin to put the restructure and reorganisation in place anyway.

'Why didn't you tell us about your doubts?' William asked.

'Tim told us if we didn't like it, we could leave,' Kate said, the skin at the opening of her blouse reddening. 'He put all our jobs at risk. In the new structure there wouldn't have been positions for us all. I have a family, a mortgage, I feared for my livelihood . . .' Her words faded.

'But your job wasn't at risk,' William said.

'Yes, it was,' Jayesh said. 'All our jobs were.'

The board members hadn't known this. Tim had kept the two groups apart and, we now learnt, cast aspersions about each to the other.

Zainab said that she too had begun to doubt the plan. 'Not just the absence of a business case; there was no contingency, no plan B.'

'We asked for more detail but never got it,' another member added.

'Yet you agreed to go ahead with the consultation,' I said.

'Yes. We completely ignored risk. We so wanted to believe Tim. But we pushed back,' William said.

'Yes, yes, absolutely,' people joined in like a chorus.

'We may have pushed back, but in the end we were pushed over,' Amber stated.

No one spoke for a moment. A window rattled in the wind and the clocks ticked, each telling different times.

I smiled at Amber, grateful for her willingness to confront their part in the disarray. To build on this, I asked them to identify the stress that had tipped them over the edge. Although some people acknowledged that they could easily retreat into a mad place again if they didn't understand what they'd done, others became defensive: they'd only behaved like this briefly, because of Tim, and they'd reacted brilliantly when he left by stopping the consultation. Unconsciously a hidden battle raged between a 'basic assumption' state of mind and what Bion called a 'work group', when teams are sane and on-task.

I stuck with it. 'Whatever Tim did, you also set him up by charging him with organisational transformation at great haste. You cast aside even the possibility of any downside of the restructure and reorganisation. You insisted everything was good and only good, and must happen today, if not yesterday.'

Zainab talked about her aversion to risk; she'd worried that her qualms about the plan stemmed from this, so didn't say anything that might derail change.

'Or put yourself at odds with the rest of the group?' I asked.

'I suppose so,' she said. 'Now I can't believe I didn't stand up and say no.'

We took a break. Leaving the room and moving around dispersed the tension a little. When we resumed, William told the senior team he understood them not speaking out and telling the board what was going on. 'We made it pretty impossible. In your place, I would've done the same thing.' A few other members agreed. It was a shift.

Eleanor said that in her enthralment, she'd refused to let anyone put her off or slow things down. 'I pretty much closed my ears and eyes.' She twirled her wedding ring again.

'Thank you for acknowledging that,' Amber said.

'It was like an adrenaline fix – it beat any soap opera,' Nigel admitted. 'If I'm honest, part of me enjoyed that.'

I told them about 'basic assumption pairing', emphasising that the problem wasn't the pair or the excitement, but losing touch with reality and avoiding the hard work of the present tense. They could see they'd contributed to Tim's behaviour in this way, perhaps putting intolerable pressure on him. No one had mentioned that the organisation could have collapsed. Or had I got that wrong?

'No, you're not wrong,' William said. 'Of course, we could have collapsed.'

'Still could,' Eleanor added.

They agreed that Eleanor would hold a meeting with all the staff and apologise for putting them through such turmoil.

She'd confirm that the consultation remained on hold, and the restructure and reorganisation would go ahead at a slower pace and involve staff in the process. They also decided to advertise for a new chief executive.

'I'm really sorry.' Eleanor looked around the room. 'I'm sorry to you all.'

The wind had stopped and between bursts of rain, flickers of sun lit the room. I thought of the weather of our minds – storms, rain, hail, sunshine – that, like a typical April day, can change so fast.

Zainab encompassed us all in her gaze. 'Do we stand a chance?'

Did they? Some had tried to avoid it, but in the end everyone in the room had taken responsibility for their part in what had happened. I recalled my slips and slides in and out of sanity. The insane parts in the background of our individual minds or the collective mind in a group, waits to pounce. In the same way individuals move between the split and simplistic and the more integrated and realistic positions, teams go between more or less sane and insane states of mind. And as reflection on this can accelerate individual development, so it can with teams. I'd gained confidence in my ability to recover my own mind. I felt hopeful they would too.

once I confirm that the [illegible] confirmed [illegible]
the temperature and [illegible] would [illegible] been slower
[illegible] and [illegible] the [illegible]. That [illegible] the
[illegible] executives.

I'm really sorry. [illegible]
[illegible] at all.

He [illegible] stopped and [illegible] Bust [illegible]
[illegible] the [illegible] center [illegible]
[illegible]
[illegible]

[illegible]
[illegible]

[illegible] and [illegible]
[illegible] for their part [illegible]
[illegible] and [illegible]
[illegible] the background of [illegible]
[illegible] wants [illegible]
[illegible]
[illegible]
[illegible]
[illegible]
[illegible]
[illegible]

11

The Poison of Envy

I heard a slight rush in Derek's breathing. Chief executive of a private coaching company, he'd rung to tell me they'd lost a bid for a three-year contract to coach leaders for a multinational corporation.

'It was bigger by miles than anything we've done before. Winning it would've secured our future for several years,' he said. 'I don't know if we can survive now.'

Most of the company's work had come from local authorities, but financial cuts meant this was drying up and they urgently needed to break into the private sector.

I listened to what sounded like a chair scraping against the floor and imagined this large, slightly ungainly fifty-something man, standing up and pacing around his office. I was running a workshop with his senior team the following week and we agreed to use it to explore what had happened.

I'd known Derek from his previous company but hadn't met the other four team members – Steve, Alan, Declan and Maria. Steve, the only one with tendering experience had, at Derek's request, led on the bid. He worked part-time for the company and the rest of the time ran his own business.

At the workshop, Steve explained they'd come second in the tendering process which, given they were unknown, was a remarkable achievement according to the head of human resources. She'd said they should bid for other work coming up soon and offered to meet Steve at their headquarters in Berlin to give him detailed feedback, but Derek had said no.

'Too bloody right I did,' Derek growled, tapping the side of his left nostril as he inhaled loudly. 'We'd spent way too much on this already.'

'It was one day and a cheap flight to meet people and get invaluable information. I still can't believe you refused,' Steve said.

The two men glared at one another. Derek inhaled again. The buttons of his pale blue shirt strained against his stomach. Steve half stood, then sat back down. Mid-forties, small and neat, he pushed back the flop of blonde hair falling over his high forehead.

'I totally prioritised this,' he said. 'I moved all my private clients, put in crazy hours, worked evenings and weekends.'

He listed what had gone wrong: Derek had said he'd get references for the bid but hadn't; the team were meant to provide key information and complete required proforma (such as the anti-slavery statement) but hadn't; and on the final Friday, the administrator missed the deadline for the courier (this was before the days of online bidding).

'I came this close to quitting.' Steve held his forefinger and thumb a millimetre apart. He'd gone home, drank too much wine, given up. But the next morning he picked himself up, spent three hours ringing around until he found people to take the bids to two different European cities in time for the Monday morning deadline.

'You arranged that yourself?' Alan asked.

'Who did you think arranged it?' Steve said. He scanned the room. 'I got zero support with the whole bid. None of you—'

'Oh, for fuck's sake, you made a ridiculously huge deal

about it,' Derek interrupted, his face red, his fists clenched. 'The bid wasn't even that good. And when you told me about the interview, I was pretty appalled at some of your answers to the questions.'

The others turned to the window, suddenly interested in the nothing that was going on outside. An unseen tap dripped.

'I. Am. Not. Taking. Any. More,' Steve spat.

Would what I do if he stormed out? Resigned? A moment passed, then another.

Steve jerked his forefinger at Derek. 'You just can't help yourself, can you? You know how hard I worked, that I put everything into this but not even a thank you. If the bid was that bad why didn't you do it? Why didn't you go to the interview?'

I didn't understand why Derek hadn't thanked him. And why he hadn't let him go to Berlin to meet the company and get feedback. I tried to gather my thoughts, but the continuing skirmish between Derek and Steve drummed them out. Alan, Declan and Maria sat mesmerised. To take the focus off the two men, I asked the others their views. They claimed the bid had nothing to do with them. I challenged this: as part of the senior leadership team it must have something to do with them.

Maria spoke up. 'You were so keen, Steve, so totally focused on the bid. You knew exactly what needed to be done. I didn't see what I could add. And you didn't seem to want us involved—'

'That's not true,' Steve interrupted.

'When I suggested something near the beginning, you turned your nose up—'

'Yes, about how to structure the bid. Sorry. But I've done loads of successful bids. I didn't need help with that. I needed the information I asked for.'

'You looked down at our inexperience, Steve, so why would we bother?' Declan asked.

'You didn't need experience, you just needed to help me.' Steve looked exasperated.

'Did you think what it was like for us?' Alan asked. 'We're not your secretaries.'

Steve leaned forward. 'Get real. With the incredibly tight deadline, you think I should have worried about your feelings?'

'You're a fucking prima donna,' Derek bellowed, tiny droplets of spit following his words.

'Fuck this.' Steve half rose again from his chair.

'Enough,' I said. 'Derek, Steve, stop.'

We took a break. I hoped after time out they'd return to an adult meeting rather than a kindergarten. It wasn't only the squabbling and viciousness; there was something mean in the atmosphere. Associations drifted across my mind: mean, ungrateful, ungenerous. Envy. Of course. Derek hadn't thanked Steve. I imagined the ugliness of envy shoving aside gratitude and stopping him in his tracks. In a coaching session, I could have tackled it directly with him, but I couldn't do that in the group.

We explored Steve's approach to the bid. The others couldn't comprehend why he'd invited people from outside the company to form part of the project team, reducing their profit. Steve looked incredulous as he explained that an international bid needs an international team. The more they asked him, the more the gap between his experience and theirs stood out.

I commented on the difficulty of depending so much on Steve in this new area of their work.

'I would never have thought of approaching the bid like you did,' Declan said. 'If I'd written it, I don't suppose we'd have even been shortlisted, let alone come second.'

Steve touched Declan's shoulder. 'Thank you.'

'I'm embarrassed about how much I don't know,' Maria said. Steve smiled at her.

'I wonder if you were envious of Steve's skills and knowledge?' I asked.

'Rubbish. We could all have written the bid,' Derek snarled.

'Didn't you hear what I just said?' Declan asked. Maria and Alan joined in, the three of them now willing to speak out against Derek.

'Well, you're going to have to learn fast, because it's the future.' Derek drew himself up and pulled in his stomach.

They turned to the window again. I imagined their fear of being incompetent, unable to learn fast enough or well enough and publicly failing. They were used to the privacy of coaching, not the public exposure of bidding with its stark result for all to see.

Derek rounded on Steve. 'We needed to win this.'

Steve sucked his teeth.

'It's not his fault,' Declan said. 'And our behaviour didn't help.'

'Actually, I think you sabotaged the bid,' I said.

'But that would be perverse.' Maria looked aghast. 'The company needed this project and we need the company.'

'It *is* perverse,' I agreed. 'That doesn't mean it didn't happen.'

'Bloody hell,' Alan muttered.

'At least we now have a template for doing bids,' Steve said.

'And we're known by the multinational,' Alan added.

'Sabotage is too hot a topic?' I asked.

'Shit,' Declan said.

We tried to make sense of the sabotage: how envy and destructiveness had taken over, blinding them to their behaviour. Derek didn't say anything. Maria asked Steve if he could teach them about the process, so in the future they could do their share of writing bids. Glancing at Derek, Steve agreed. They laughed and joked for the first time. At the end of the workshop they went to the pub together.

It was a good outcome, yet I remained uneasy; if Derek didn't change his behaviour and show some appreciation, I doubted Steve would hang around for long. The next day I emailed Derek, suggesting some individual coaching sessions to support him as he repositioned the company and they all adapted. He agreed, although only found a date two months ahead, and then only if I came into central London so he could fit it between other meetings.

We met at the Russell Hotel. The lounge, with its low hum of voices, comfy armchairs and sofas and discreet waiting staff, transported me to another era. Only the bar at the end of the room seemed of this century.

Derek arrived a few minutes late and joined me by the window in the far corner. We ordered drinks. He told me Steve had resigned and left last week.

'We'd only got a few sandwiches for his leaving do,' Derek said, 'so the administrator produced an old bottle of wine from the back of the stationery cupboard. Turned out it was off – pure vinegar – completely undrinkable.' He uttered a sound between a sneer and a giggle.

They had successfully spoilt Steve's pleasure in his leaving do and ensured he'd go feeling bad. Spoiling is a typical response to envy: keying cars, for example, achieves nothing except to spoil the owner's pleasure. Derek's blindness to his envy made it corrosive. He seemed unaware that his inability to appreciate Steve left his envy free to spread its poison; and that if he couldn't curb it, he risked losing the other staff too.

I asked him why Steve got under his skin. It was his arrogance about the bid, Derek said. True, I said, yet look how impressed the multinational had been. Impressed doesn't cut it, he said. They hadn't won. He repeated what he'd said at the workshop: they could all have written the bid.

'Perhaps you were both arrogant? Steve in thinking he was the only one who could write a bid and you in thinking that anyone can write a bid.'

'It's not a real skill. Not like being able to run a company or being a brilliant coach.'

'You seem determined that Steve's expertise brought no real value.'

A waitress cleared the table.

'OK, OK,' Derek muttered when she'd gone. 'I could have thanked him, if that's what you mean. Would've stuck in my throat, but I could. Maybe he wouldn't have left. Or at least would have taught us about tendering before he did.'

'He didn't do that?'

Derek shook his head. 'Can't really blame him.' He smiled, looking more relaxed as his enmity loosened and he saw Steve's point of view.

We talked about whether the company should try for these large time-consuming bids, that probably wouldn't yield results for a while, or whether to concentrate on smaller bids that paid less but were quicker to do and would produce results sooner. Derek insisted they had to go for the big projects, the 'large bucks'.

I wondered if vanity, as well as anxiety about survival, drove him.

Laughter from a nearby table caught my attention; I noticed a father and daughter chatting amiably together. I recalled Derek telling me about his daughter's passion for swimming and all the early morning lessons and weekend competitions he took her to. He beamed when I mentioned this; she'd just got into the junior national team.

'I'm so proud of her. I don't know where she gets her love of exercise from,' he laughed, patting his stomach.

'You helped her.'

He grinned. 'I'd do anything for her.'

In a sudden movement, Derek glanced at his watch and, standing up, said he had another meeting. He apologised, told me he'd ring to arrange another session and left. I sat in the armchair, thrown by the abrupt ending. If he really had to leave early because of another meeting, wouldn't he have mentioned it at the start? Maybe softening towards Steve and talking about his daughter had reminded Derek of his capacity for love and generosity. Was he rushing away from that memory, that knowledge?

Derek didn't get in touch. I resisted the urge to prompt him. I imagined his internal battle. On one side, his daughter, his loving feelings and generosity; on the other, his mean envy and viciousness. Sometimes envy motivates, rather than disfigures us, but that wasn't the case for Derek. For him, it seemed like a character in his internal world that commanded his loyalty. A presence all the more potent for being unknown to him. That side of him wouldn't want me around.

At Christmas I received a card. 'Sorry I didn't get in touch. It's been tough but the company is doing well and I'm learning to control that temper of mine.'

I thought about bosses unencumbered by much narcissism or envy, who enjoy developing others and seeing them shine. Their generosity benefits their staff and the atmosphere of their workplaces. Envious bosses, like envious parents, feel more provoked than proud when their staff or children outshine them. Generosity isn't possible and instead meanness spills over and bosses or parents put their staff or children down.

Controlling his outbursts, while remaining unacquainted with the envy behind them, was probably as much as Derek could do. It would certainly help. It may even lessen his disconnection from those he envied since, if he didn't fear his anger, he might be able to get closer to them. That in turn could lessen envy's hold on him. In this way, managing his temper might dispel some of his destructiveness. Perhaps it was good enough.

12

Turning a Blind Eye

In the immediate aftermath of the fatal Boeing 737 Max plane crashes in October 2018 and March 2019, the company insisted the plane was safe. After the second crash, Boeing's chief executive rang President Donald Trump to confirm this, and the US Federal Administration Authority (FAA) issued a 'Continued Airworthiness Notification'.

Three days later, the FAA found links between both accidents and 737 Max planes were grounded worldwide. By April, Boeing admitted there had been problems with the 'Maneuvering Characteristics Augmentation System' (MCAS).

In January 2020, the *New York Times*, accessing previously confidential information, ran a story about a crash of the 737 Max's predecessor in 2009 in the Netherlands. Nine people died. There were several similarities between the 2009 and the 2018 and 2019 crashes. All three involved a malfunction in the automated system and, in all three, Boeing had failed to give pilots information that could have helped them deal with the problem. On each occasion Boeing tried, at least initially, to blame the pilots, claiming they hadn't reacted correctly to the malfunction.

In fact, Boeing knew about a possible system fault from the investigation in 2009. The aviation expert commissioned by the Dutch Safety Board found that while pilot error contributed to the accident, Boeing's high-risk design choices and questionable safety assessments played a significant part. The expert had criticised Boeing for trying to deflect from their failure to take the possible system fault seriously, by telling pilots to be more vigilant. But under pressure from the American investigation team, which included representatives from Boeing and federal safety officials, the study remained under wraps and was only released after the *New York Times* investigation in 2020.

It's clear that in designing the 737 Max, Boeing knew about possible technical issues but turned away from that knowledge. It's easy to imagine why the company hid its technical problems. They aren't alone; time and again companies and governments turn a blind eye to difficulties, choosing short-term gains over ethical values and the expense of correcting problems.

To some extent, we all do this: how many of us believe in the importance of taxation yet pay the decorator or builder in cash? Saving ourselves money, we turn a blind eye to our double standards.

Our propensity for turning a blind eye isn't only motivated by money and profit; frequently it's driven by anxiety, which steers our choice not to see or think about the harm our blindness causes. Anxiety, usually unconscious, can, for instance, propel us to turn a blind eye to the damage of our addiction or of a bad relationship. We know it and at the same time, turn away from our knowledge. Preferring mental somersaults to the truth, we add denial to the defensive mix, telling ourselves that not acting, not speaking out, or not looking, is no big deal.

The psychoanalyst John Steiner says turning a blind eye takes advantage of *chance* and *collusion*. For a long time, many of us clung to the chance that normal shifts in weather patterns caused climate changes. We went along with this notion, downplaying the facts. Some of us still do.

On a smaller scale, I frequently hear staff bemoan the fact that managers turn a blind eye to poor performance or unacceptable behaviour. Wishing to escape the difficult and time-consuming task of tackling a problem, they hold on to the slim chance that an individual will change, and the issue resolve itself. Sometimes turning a blind eye becomes so ingrained, an entire organisation colludes in looking away from problems.

A chief executive came to see me after his company lost a major client because one of his staff hadn't provided a good enough service. The chief executive had heard rumours and been told directly about the problems but, hating conflict, had chosen to believe the rumours were exaggerated. When the client left, the staff member was sacked. If the chief executive had faced the issue, the company could have retained the client, and might have been able to help the staff member improve their work.

On another occasion, when the head of division in a company died unexpectedly, his senior team asked me to meet with them. They told me the junior staff were heartbroken. A distraught intern had told one of them that she used to do the head of division's shopping. I felt uncomfortable, especially when other senior team members revealed that since his death, they'd heard many similar tales – nothing illicit – but overstepping the normal boundaries between managers and staff. Junior staff and interns had done shopping, baby-sitting, hunting down scarce tickets for concerts for him.

I told them to inform a senior leader. It was gossip, they said; they couldn't slander the dead head of division with gossip. Worried about what else might emerge, I reminded them of the Jimmy Savile story which had just broken. The next day they told the chief executive.

Several organisations I have worked with, when faced with crippling financial cuts, have necessarily watered down their services to save money. They tread a difficult path between staying afloat and reducing quality. But if quality reduces to the point where services or products are no longer safe, the line is crossed and the organisation has succumbed to the dangers of turning a blind eye.

At its worst, turning a blind eye perverts the truth, corrupts organisations and individuals and causes catastrophic damage. More mundanely, it causes neglect and undermines us and our workplaces.

Hoping for quick rewards, an easier life and less anxiety, we all look away at times. Yet, just as what is repressed returns, the issues we turn away from rebound. And, when they do, they are fortified by their time spent festering out of sight.

One of the most damaging, insidious effects of turning a blind eye is our loss of curiosity: we dampen it down in order not to see. Without it, both individuals and organisations cease to develop and cannot thrive. Instead of moving forward with questions and sight, we stand still with blind disinterest.

Curiosity generates the conditions that enable us to go further and face the truth: about ourselves, our world and our workplaces. Without that, we make the wrong decisions and take the wrong actions or prevaricate with no actions.

Truly facing ourselves takes time and courage. As Steiner says, 'the fact that we do sometimes face the truth [about ourselves] however imperfectly, is a considerable achievement'.

The mechanism of turning a blind eye seduces us in a variety of wily ways. Limiting it involves vigilance, actively encouraging sight over blindness, and creating environments in and out of work, where truth and inquisitiveness prosper.

13

Repeating Patterns

It was the fifth weekly session with a team in an NHS adolescent unit and still they cried. Every session some staff – the individuals varied – were in tears from the beginning to the end of our hour together. I felt soaked through, wrung out with the emotions that seeped into me from them. Distress, anger and, this week, I sensed shame. It produced a physical reaction in me; my skin crawled, I felt dirty, I wanted a shower.

The NHS trust had asked me to work with the team a few months after suspending Martin, their manager, for alleged bullying. An investigation was under way. The picture the team painted of Martin made me think of the Gestapo; someone who enjoyed the opportunity to unleash his sadism. He'd made life hell, they said, especially for the nurses. He hadn't dared with the doctors. You never knew when you'd become the target. When you did, the full force of his rage and criticism turned on you. He'd bark orders and then shout at you for following them. If you reminded him that he'd told you to do whatever it was, he denied his instruction. He constantly scorned your work with the young people, until you believed you were incompetent and stupid.

I felt for the team; they seem so broken, so hurt. But I was beginning to question the one-sidedness of their story, in which they were always innocent victims. Perhaps the sense of shame this week suggested that at some level the team knew they'd contributed to what happened with Martin.

We talked about how long the bullying had gone on for. Being unable to stop it sooner, I said, must have added to their pain.

'No one could have stopped it sooner,' Linda, a senior nurse, said sharply, her matronly shoe tapping the floor. Her tone surprised me. Linda was a mother-figure in the team. She often brought in chocolates for them and was always the one to offer me a drink.

'But maybe if—' Paul, the new consultant psychiatrist, ventured. He fiddled with his red tie which matched the red laces in his dark blue shoes.

Linda, her hand raised in a stop sign, cut him off. 'You weren't here, you don't know. It was impossible to stop it before.' Her legs crossed, her right foot bounced up and down. A strand of light brown hair escaped from the band keeping it off her face.

'We did stop it in the end,' Carmen, the consultant psychologist said, in her Spanish accent. 'That letter we wrote to the trust.' She looked down. 'Perhaps we should have done that earlier.'

Implying that the team might bear some responsibility for what had ensued indicated a turning point. After the session, I walked back down the corridor. The young people's bedrooms and lounge were on the other side of the double doors on my right. I could hear grunts and swearing, the mandatory language of adolescence. At the reception the administrator buzzed me out of the locked doors.

The following week, Carmen voiced her concerns about a new patient. Linda agreed with her. They cited examples of the boy's worrying behaviour. Paul listened attentively and offered to meet with them both that afternoon. Their collaboration and focus on their work shifted the mood. The tears were brief this time, coming only towards the end of the session when someone asked what was happening with Martin's job.

Stepping into the room a week later, Linda instantly raised her hand in the stop sign. She asked me to wait outside as their meeting hadn't finished. I stood in the corridor looking at the noticeboard with photos of staff. The years dropped away and I was back at school, waiting in trepidation outside the head teacher's office. Ten minutes passed before Linda called me in. A few people muttered 'hello'.

'How are things?' I asked. Someone mumbled 'OK'. They usually gave me a brief summary of the state of the unit, the patients and the team. No one made eye contact with me. I tried asking how the week had been. Another 'OK'. Another silence. Paul glanced at me. He seemed embarrassed. The silence continued. I felt wrong-footed.

'What's going on?' I asked. No answer. My eyes landed on a small beetle, crawling millimetre by millimetre across the carpet, taking long detours around a slightly raised or uneven patch. However slowly, at least the beetle was moving and making progress. I felt a surge of irritation. What *was* going on?

Carmen broke the silence. 'There's a *h*uge elephant in the room,' she said, her guttural 'h' underscoring the word. They'd been discussing what they wanted to leave behind when the unit moved premises. My sessions were mentioned. Some staff complained that I make them talk about Martin, while they want to move on. What had gone on was irrelevant for new staff so, some thought, they should leave the sessions behind.

I wanted to say fine, we can end our sessions when they moved premises next month. In fact, why not end them now? I didn't want to work with them anyway. Who would? They could go to hell. Hearing my internal dialogue, I recognised my wish to retaliate, to reject them as they were rejecting me. The strength of my feeling, and my wish to be cruel to them, surprised me. I felt ashamed, although I knew my feelings were probably an unconscious communication from the team.

Something clicked: they'd found another bully. Me. In their eyes, I'd replaced Martin. I'd become a tyrannical figure who they felt pushed them around and made them feel powerless. Like Martin. The last pieces of the jigsaw puzzle fell into place and I saw the shape and form of their unconscious pattern. Firstly, they identified a bully. Next, the bullying, whether real or perceived, became intolerable. Step three, they got rid of the bully as fast as possible. First Martin; now me.

My understanding helped me hold back my anger. As much as I wanted to, leaving at this moment would only repeat the pattern. I told them they could stop the sessions whenever they wanted.

'We don't all want to stop,' Paul said. Carmen nodded. A clear divide stood between those for and against me.

'It's not up to us anyway,' Linda said.

'You have the choice about having these sessions,' I countered. 'I don't suppose the trust will force you to continue. And even if they do, you can change the facilitator.'

I sensed the hostility lessen as it sank in that they weren't helpless victims. They had power over me. Should I tell them about the link I'd made between what had just happened with me and what had happened with Martin? It was important but would threaten their investment in their innocence and could push them into sacking me. My heartbeat a little elevated, I took the risk and raised it. The rejections came thick and fast: 'Rubbish.' 'That's ridiculous.' 'You really don't get it.'

Eventually, Julie, a relatively new junior nurse, suggested I might have a point. She looked at me. 'I didn't – don't – want you to leave either. Sorry – I couldn't say that before.' My heartbeat slowed; maybe we'd get through this moment, past this groove of the stuck record.

Another nurse spoke up. 'I'm still upset about Martin. He never picked on me, but I saw what other people went through and somehow couldn't do anything.'

'It was for the senior staff to stop it,' Carmen said. 'We took too long. We let you all down.'

Paul, his face tilted, spoke gently. 'I get the impression Martin had a very strong hold on you all. I don't really know why.'

People glanced at each other and at Linda. No one spoke.

'We just need to move on,' Linda stated, her words like a line drawing the conversation to an end.

'Perhaps, understandably, you're trying to push your painful experiences of Martin away, in the hope they'll disappear,' I said.

'They don't though,' Carmen said.

'No, they never do,' I agreed.

They continued in this thoughtful way for the rest of the session. As we ended, Julie pointed out that no one had cried.

Session by session, through an unusually hot summer and into the winter, we returned to this theme: how and why they'd allowed Martin to have this hold on them, and their part in creating the repeated destructive pattern. They often fled from it and sometimes pressing problems with patients took priority but, beetle-like, slowly and painfully, we worked to digest what had happened. We connected it to the abuse and cruelty many of their patients had suffered and unconsciously tried to recreate in the unit. Some re-enacted their experience by inviting staff to be cruel to them. For instance, an emotionally neglected and abused boy spat at the nurses until they, like his parents, shunned him. We thought about the coat of shame hanging over the patients and the staff. Shame that had made me want a shower.

Linda maintained a fierce opposition to the connection between what had gone on with Martin and their patients' behaviour, describing it as 'fanciful', 'woolly' or reverting to repeating that they needed to move on. I often felt irritation and dislike towards her, although I recognised that she stood for something important in the team. Slowly it came to me: she represented their wish to repress painful experiences. I knew from psychoanalytic theory, my clients as well as from myself, that when experiences or events are too difficult for us to think about, we push them away, repressing them in our unconscious. But, Freud said, what gets repressed, returns. It forces its way back into the conscious mind. And so begins the pattern of what Freud called 'repetition compulsion', a damaging, destructive cycle.

A coaching client, for example, complained that all his bosses were needy and demanding, until we discovered that without knowing it, he found or provoked bosses into being like his mother. In doing this, the distressing experiences with her, which he'd tried so hard to bury, returned.

Towards the end of winter, the mood changed again. Staff were being interviewed for Martin's disciplinary inquiry. Reliving their experiences upset them. One week, Linda informed the group that after our last meeting Julie had told her she couldn't understand why people got so upset and cried so much in the sessions. Linda's voice rose fractionally as she reported Julie saying it was just a job; she – Julie – would *never* let work get to her that much. Julie's neck and cheeks turned crimson.

Another nurse turned to her. 'So you think we're pathetic?'

'No, no, it's just . . .' Julie's voice trailed off.

'I know you told me that privately, Julie,' Linda said, her voice thick with saccharin, her smile rigid, as if glued across her mouth, 'but I'm doing this in your best interests.'

My jaw clenched. Linda was Julie's mentor; if your mentor could betray your confidence, expose and humiliate you like this, how could anyone trust anyone? The hour was nearly up. I commented that while it was helpful to talk openly in sessions, people had a choice about what was public and what remained private. Some staff looked relieved; Linda, the smile replaced by a downturn of her mouth, threw me an icy look.

In March, I walked across the car park to the unit, the trees now renewed and vibrant as spring replaced the long, dreary winter. The room was empty. I arranged the chairs and cleared a couple of mugs from the floor to the table near the door. Paul arrived early and helped me stack the remaining chairs along the back wall. He told me Linda had reported him to the trust's child and adolescent mental health service manager for spending time alone with a seventeen-year-old patient in her bedroom.

'I checked on the girl,' Paul said. 'I was really worried about her escalating self-harm.' Unable to get hold of a knife in the unit, the girl had wounded the tops of her thighs by stabbing them with the lid of a biro.

He told me that when he'd started his training in psychiatry, a patient he'd assessed killed herself. He'd waited in mounting fear all morning at the subsequent inquest watching while his colleagues were interrogated. When his turn came, he stumbled on his way to the witness stand on legs that suddenly seemed unable to carry him. In fact, the coroner protected him, redirecting any difficult questions to his consultant.

'The trust wasn't found culpable, but it was terrible. I nearly quit. I found the death of this young woman – thirty years old, newly married – devastating. It shouldn't have happened. I felt so guilty. All these years later, I still wonder if I could have prevented it.'

'That must have been incredibly hard, especially at the outset of your career,' I said.

'The consultant was very supportive, everyone was. But now I'm the consultant. I'm responsible. I'm the one who would be on the witness stand and interrogated.'

'Can you talk about Linda's complaint in the session?' I asked.

'I'll try.'

I'd begun to think Paul wouldn't say anything when, towards the end of the session, he told Linda he knew she had concerns about him. The others looked surprised and confused. Linda folded her arms.

'Well . . . I . . .' she stuttered.

'What's going on? What are you talking about, Paul?' Carmen asked.

'Linda?' Paul's eyebrows raised as he gestured towards her.

'If you must know, I'm worried about your lack of boundaries. It's very important here. This is to protect you, Paul. You don't know what you'll be accused of,' Linda said.

'I think I am being accused of something,' Paul replied.

'What? What's happened?' Carmen asked again.

Paul told them.

'You should have got a nurse to go with you into her bedroom. You shouldn't have gone on your own,' Linda said.

'I know,' Paul agreed. He glanced at me, before telling them about the patient who killed herself and how he'd panicked the same thing would happen.

'I did look for you, Carmen, to talk to, but it was 6.30 and you'd gone home. You're right though, Linda, I should have taken a nurse with me.'

'Sorry I wasn't around,' Carmen said. 'But, Linda, you complained to the service manager? Why didn't you speak to Paul before formalising it?'

'I'm surprised you ask. You know we have a duty of care to the patients,' Linda said, the saccharin coating her voice again.

The nurses glanced at one another. We all knew Paul had made a mistake, but it was well intentioned. And it would have been far worse if the girl had killed herself. We knew too that he'd always have the complaint on his record. I couldn't speak for a moment; I was so angry with Linda, I feared what I'd say. It's a team, I reminded myself for the umpteenth time; Linda is part of their unconscious pattern. I found the words, suggesting that unconsciously they'd positioned Linda as the protector of standards and patient care.

'Someone's got to,' Linda said.

'Don't you all have to?' I asked.

We ended the session. Paul smiled at me as I left the room. Going down the corridor back to reception I heard a disembodied adolescent voice shouting, 'That's not allowed.' I thought of Linda's rigid rule enforcement, her 'thou shalt nots', and how they reinforced, as well as reflected, the rigidity that sometimes characterises young people's thinking. Rules can be followed or broken. The either/or simplicity requires less thinking than a more flexible, nuanced, approach.

As I wrote my notes that evening, it dawned on me that Linda had become the latest bully. How had I missed this? I'd been so focused on managing my hostility towards her, I hadn't seen the repetition staring me in the face. Martin, then me and now Linda. She put herself there by becoming the team's conscience, their berating superego. Had

Martin done that too? Had I? It might have felt that way to the team.

Another part of the jigsaw fell into place: being the 'conscience' usually feels persecutory to others and, while I was confident Paul could improve their outcomes, to date the unit only scraped by in inspections, never achieving high standards of care or results. This gave the person of 'conscience' added power, making them the perfect unconscious choice for the role of bully.

I worried that Linda, having become the bully, would soon be ousted and the process would start again. At the next session, I mentioned the link between the person who took up the conscience for the team and the one who became the bully. Apart from with Paul and Carmen, this got little traction. I persisted, focusing on how they all needed to uphold standards. After a couple of sessions, Linda began to dismount her high horse. She withdrew her complaint against Paul.

The investigation into Martin ended in May. It was inconclusive and he was 'encouraged' to take early retirement. Staff who had been around when he managed the unit were distraught; they'd waited so long for his punishment and their vindication. For a few weeks we returned to the incessant crying of our early sessions. It provided another chance to work through what had happened. Finally, they accepted that the repeated pattern of bullying was bigger than Martin: it had become embedded insidiously in the unit's culture, deep in its DNA, with roots of iron that were incredibly hard to break.

I left in October. The team hadn't pushed Linda out and, so far, hadn't produced another bully. They were doing better, although their capacity to think and digest experiences rather than push them away or enact them, remained fragile. Leaving them at this point may have been too early, but I felt unable to achieve more. Or perhaps I feared being trapped with them in the sinkhole of repetition compulsion and its unconscious impulse to repeat our repressed memories, thoughts or feelings. Sometimes the repetition carries the hope that *this* time, we'll be able to control it, master what failed us before. But the cycle goes on and we remain stuck in destructiveness that stems from – and in turn fuels – our death drive. In its hold, we neglect our constructive drive for life which, starved of our care, diminishes.

14

The Hidden Difficulties of Succession

I clambered on the train with seconds to spare. Stowing my raincoat in the luggage rack above, I flung myself into a seat by the window, looking back in relief as the train moved forward and Birmingham New Street Station disappeared.

'No need to worry about the stories in my book only showing me in a good light,' I emailed Mike Brearley. 'I've just run a session that went spectacularly wrong.'

The disastrous session was my second meeting with the staff of a department in a large charity. I'd run the first one a few months earlier. Between the two sessions, the deputy head of department resigned. The recruitment process for his successor had resulted in two front-runners, one internal and one external candidate. The interview panel agreed to appoint the external candidate. Afterwards, unbeknown to the panel, Joanna, the head of department, created a second deputy position and appointed Graham, the internal candidate. The team weren't told, there was no advertisement or selection process and, apart from with human resources, no discussion in the charity about creating a new position.

Graham was the only internal candidate; other staff hadn't

applied because the international travel involved put the job out of reach for many, especially those with children. Graham had also worried about the travel, but when Joanna created the post for him, she made it UK only.

I'd already heard something of the shenanigans from the departing deputy head of department, when Joanna emailed me, telling me about the appointments. I found the corruption of the recruitment process staggering, especially since the charity had been set up by philanthropists to do good in the world.

By the time the workshop took place, the previous deputy had left, Graham had started, and the external candidate would be joining in two months. As in the previous session, the task was to help staff function as well as possible by thinking about their dynamics and the impact of their work.

We had two and a half hours. I didn't know what would be possible or helpful to explore about the recruitment process or whether anyone would raise the subject. I gave them opportunities, but it remained unspoken, the silence hovering like a tidal wave threatening to wash over the room.

The words came just before the end of the session. The team had been in small groups proposing changes to ways of working that would help the department. The penultimate group said they wanted more transparency, including in recruitment. Here it is, I thought.

Before I could ask the other groups for their comments, Graham jumped in and began giving feedback for the last group. I hesitated, aware of how difficult this must be for him and unsure what to do. Should I stop him or let him continue since his group did need to give feedback? Struggling to think, I did the latter. It was a mistake. Compelled no doubt by anxiety, Graham filled the time with his drawn-out feedback. Paralysed, I didn't stop him. When he finished, I asked for comments or questions. Nothing. Seven minutes to go. I asked where the session had left them. Two minutes passed. Should I say something? No, it was too late. But if I didn't speak, I'd be colluding with Joanna and Graham's attempt to bury the corruption.

'I think when you mentioned transparency in recruitment you were talking about a recent recruitment process, involving people sitting in the room,' I said. The air thickened, the wave threatened.

I continued, 'If you can't find a way of talking about this, it will paralyse you.'

A woman rambled incoherently, anxiously filling the space again. A man cut across her, speaking directly to me.

'How could you? How could you bring this up with five minutes to go and leave us like this?' I explained my dilemma: whether I should say something so close to the end of the session or collude with them in leaving it unspoken.

Joanna, sitting opposite me, her face flushed with fury, spat, 'But *five* minutes. We've got *five* minutes to go.'

We agreed to extend the session by fifteen minutes.

Joanna's rage turned to the team. 'You lot have been appalling to Graham since he got the job. You ganged up on him. It's outrageous, completely unprofessional.' I understood this as an unconscious projection to the staff of her own outrageous, unprofessional behaviour. No one made eye contact. The hands inched round the clock.

'It's not personal,' a man said. 'Sorry, Graham. We know how good you are. We're lucky to have you as a deputy. It's about the process.' Graham nodded.

Someone suggested we arrange another session. I agreed. The fifteen minutes up, I wished them well and said goodbye. Staff trickled out of the room. Several came up and thanked me. I waited for Joanna, resisting my wish to flee. She was the last to leave. Walking down the corridor with me she let rip again: what did I think I was doing; how could I do that to Graham? I said I felt bad about that.

We found Graham in his office and I apologised for putting him in this difficult position.

'You did me a favour. You burst the huge boil. At least now it's out in the open.'

Joanna calmed down and we agreed to have another session soon. Relief flooded through me.

On the train though, I wondered if I'd got it terribly wrong. It was important to expose the corruption and it would have been inappropriate for me to say anything before the team brought it up, but the timing left them to deal with the tidal wave long after I'd gone. In attempting to counter this by extending the session, I'd enacted the broken boundaries of the recruitment process and the disarray it created. I shouldn't have allowed the last group to metaphorically grab the microphone. If I'd just mentioned, gestured to the recruitment process in response to the penultimate group's feedback, rather than rushing in headlong, perhaps I could have shown that I wasn't colluding, yet not left them with an indigestible ending.

I was used to working with the perils of succession in organisations. I knew the vulnerability it creates, particularly when senior leaders are involved. Often organisations become unbalanced. While most right themselves, some tip over.

I recalled the senior leadership team I'd worked with just after their admired and loved leader of many years retired. As the date approached, he'd picked fights with everyone, refused to do a proper handover and left an indecipherable mess of notes behind like a large lump of excrement stuck in the toilet. The organisation had nearly gone under and the leadership team were at loggerheads. We came to understand that in his acute anxiety about retirement, unconsciously the leader had tried to bring the organisation down rather than see it continue and change without him.

On another occasion, a man who'd resigned as chief executive of a small organisation after just eight months – a post he'd been excited to get – came to see me wanting to make sense of his upsetting and confusing experience. Having welcomed him warmly, the board of the organisation then blocked him; they checked every idea he had and anything he tried to do with the former chief executive. She'd led the organisation for decades; it was her life. Although people found her iron-fist control infuriating, she worked harder than anyone and was effective.

We realised that beneath the delight in her departure, the board dreaded losing the person they depended on. Without doing the psychological work required to understand this and let go, the organisation clung onto her and she to it. The disconnect between the board and staff's words of welcome and their actions made it impossible for my client. He'd been right to leave. In this circumstance, the first successor could only pave the way for the second one to succeed.

Another client talked to me about taking over as director of a training programme. As part of the transition, she and the existing director had agreed that she would lead the next programme. It hadn't happened; apart from delegating small administrative tasks, the existing director continued to lead. My client blamed herself for failing to take her authority.

As a teenager she'd retreated from the aggression adolescents need to take their place in the world – the process of generational succession that involves adolescents pushing ahead, disregarding the pain it might cause their parents. Her parents were elderly, and her fear of their frailty meant she'd shied away from this developmental step. As an adult she still struggled to claim her place. This time though, the problem wasn't hers alone; she and the existing director needed to manage succession together. As with adolescents and their parents, it was a two-way process – one had to take hold, the other had to let go.

The train passed through Milton Keynes. I thought of the murky, at times dirty, manoeuvrings that can occur during succession. The back stabbings, sucking up, the disingenuous alliances.

Succession can cause fractures in both organisations and families. In the family feuds over inheritance reignite rivalries in an unconscious contest over who is the legitimate inheritor, the chief mourner, and who will continue the family name with all that it represents. In the workplace, the battle centres on which staff member the outgoing leader favours, who will inherit the title, who is charged with continuing – or revitalising – the brand.

Succession in organisations is vital for renewal, but like all substantial change, it provokes resistance and brings loss, whether of a person, or an era. The destabilising effects of these hidden difficulties didn't normally throw me. This time though, corruption joined the complex, crowded scene and I'd lost my balance.

What had made Joanna succumb to inequitable and unethical behaviour? From a small working-class town in Scotland, she'd been mediocre at school, but got a place at university, the first in her family to go into higher education. She'd told me that getting the job in the charity, with its upper-class Oxbridge senior leaders, exceeded all her expectations. She loved it, although she always felt an outsider and often worried that she'd make a faux pas because she didn't understand the informal rules and etiquette staff and board members played by. Graham, on the other hand, had been to public school and Cambridge University. His wife, a dame, sat on the board of a charity in the same field. With powerful connections, and the confidence and entitlement of the British upper class, his insider status was indisputable.

I wondered if deep down Joanna believed that the upper class are born to rule and her leadership position was illegitimate. Maybe the act of granting Graham the job, and so making him beholden to her, gave her greater security. With him as her deputy, she'd have access to his powerful connections and perhaps, she believed, be closer to his social class.

Why had Graham gone along with this though? I could only assume his ambition got the better of him. Perhaps he found his wife's greater success painful and this was a chance to catch up a little. Even more puzzling was human resources' acquiescence, unless, that is, this backhanded way of recruiting had happened before and was accepted within the culture of the charity.

I knew from the atmosphere in the session, and the words individuals muttered to me at the end, that the team were furious. When the recruitment process was finally mentioned, someone had asked what the external deputy was like. I imagined their anxiety, along with hope and excitement, as they waited for him to start; their curiosity about his take on Graham's appointment, whether the three of them would get on and how things would change. They must also have wondered whether staff favoured by Joanna and the former deputy would retain their privilege or if those previously overlooked might now enjoy a new standing.

Our focus on succession planning and how to ensure a continuance of the skills, qualities and leadership capacity is important yet misses so much. It overlooks the hidden difficulties, the unspoken, unconscious issues that load this key organisational moment. Under the weight of these issues, succession is fraught and too frequently fails.

I was right to worry about the session: I never heard from the charity again. Perhaps if I'd reacted differently, not allowed the tidal wave to flood them, Joanna would have invited me back. As it was, I'd made it too hard for her. Perhaps for Graham too, who now had to contend with hostility from the team and, if people learnt how he'd obtained his promotion, from the wider organisation. He'd also have to face his guilt at his own ruthless collusion with the corruption.

As I was writing this chapter, the 2020 US presidential election was taking place. President Trump's refusal to concede exemplified the raw reaction succession can evoke. To avoid the insufferable injury defeat would cause his excessive narcissism, he conjured up conspiracy theories and, with increasing paranoia, accused the Democrats of 'stealing' the election from him. Not from the Republicans, but from him. It was personal. As Joanna saw her own bad behaviour in the team, Trump saw in the Democrats his own proclivity to cheating and corruption. His inability to manage himself in this situation took away any semblance of his ability to do his job and act for the good of the country. Abdicating their own responsibility, senior Republicans stood by, actively supporting him in whipping up further division and suspicion.

Joanna was far from Trump, but she too lost her ground and her sight. Normal rules and ethics lost relevance in her private battle between her destructiveness and constructiveness and, at least for a while, her destructiveness got the upper hand.

15

Losing Agency

'What's happened to your muscles?' I asked. Fifteen pairs of eyes looked at me dully, uncomprehending. It was as though I'd entered a hospital ward or care home for the elderly, where both bodies and minds were in stasis. Yet I was in a university, a place of youth and energy, a place where identities are formed and futures invented.

I'd come here every month for eighteen months, to meet with the staff of student support services. A year ago they'd been relocated and split up: student advice and disability support in one building, the careers service in another and the counselling service in a third. Six months later, the university announced a major restructuring. Most of the team recoiled in dread as memories of the last restructuring, less than four years ago, flooded back.

This time was as bad. The torturous process saw dates and procedures constantly changed. At one point, the team heard on the grapevine that the counselling service might be outsourced. When they asked their boss, Andrew, about this, he said a tendering process was about to begin. They don't want us, the team told me. We may not have jobs in a couple of months, and no one cares.

The 'muscles' session was during the long wait for a verdict on their future. Their listlessness suffused the room.

'How are things?' I asked.

'You know.'

'I know how they were a month ago, but not now.'

'The same.'

'What's the impact on you?'

'You know.'

We talked about the lack of feedback from Andrew. I suggested they nudge him.

'Yes, yes, we'll do that,' someone said.

'You could ask him to tell you when he'll realistically have news about the service and your jobs,' I said.

'Oh, that's a really good idea,' someone else remarked. 'The *realistic* time, is that what you said?'

I felt elevated as, despite my banal comments, they clung to each word as though I'd become super bright and intelligent. It gave me a momentary glow, quickly followed by discomfort. I knew my new status was the rosy reflection from a distorted looking glass. I wasn't superwoman and they weren't insipid and dense, with no ideas, or thoughts.

They relayed, as they had every month, the missed deadlines for each part of the tendering process and the number of times Andrew cancelled meetings, as he spent more and more time off site. Andrew had become conspicuous by his absence. When the team needed him most, like the rest of the senior leaders, he'd distanced himself and become unreliable. No one gave the team information or support; no one absorbed some of their anxiety by allowing them to be more dependent during the time of uncertainty.

I'd seen the team depressed, upset, thoughtful, humorous. But I'd never seen this passivity. Its physical sensation had led me to ask about their muscles. I followed it with an explanation: 'You're so limp. I've never seen you like this.'

Like a light going on, electricity pulsed through the room.

They sat up straighter, did arm thrusts, laughed. Perhaps it was my reference to their bodies that helped switch the oxygen supply back on. As they came back to life, they realised they'd cut off from their feelings and concern towards the students.

'I'm so pleased when students don't turn up,' a counsellor said.

'Yesterday a girl in her first year came to see me in a complete state,' one of the advisors said. 'She'd been kicked out of home – her family have disowned her. She'd got nowhere to go, and the exams are next week. All I could think was thank God I can pass this on to the accommodation office. The truth is, I couldn't wait to see the back of her.'

I suggested it was hard to be caring towards the students when the team felt so uncared for themselves.

I pondered the apparent absence of the university's concern and compassion towards their staff. I knew the major changes in higher education, including its funding, meant that being a senior leader was harder than ever, but nonetheless, they seemed to have lost sight of staff morale and engagement.

By the following month, the counselling team had been reprieved: the tenders from external providers were too expensive, so for now the university had decided to keep the in-house service. The whole team was relieved, but celebrations were subdued as the bad taste from their poor treatment remained. One of them had already taken early retirement; another declined to renew his contract.

We worked on their recovery. When I asked them how they could get the care and support they should expect and needed to do their jobs, they argued with me. They couldn't get it, they said. How, after everything, could I think they should trust the university? The rebuttal signalled that I'd become their normally good and trusted consultant again, rather than a magical figure who would solve everything for them.

My short-lived elevation, and their lacklustre floppiness in the previous session, reflected their retreat to an unhealthily dependent state of mind. 'Dependency' is one of the 'basic assumptions' described by Wilfred Bion. Always present in the backwaters of our minds, these states commonly come to the fore under stress. In basic assumption dependency, teams unconsciously operate under the assumption that while they may go through the motions of their official tasks, their overriding purpose is to find a leader to depend on.

Excessive dependency reduces intelligence, wit, thought, will and determination. Yet it can be attractive. At the beginning of my analysis I yearned to be looked after. To my astonishment, I wanted to collapse. I'd had to grow up too fast and wanted to return to an infantile state. I didn't want agency and autonomy; I wanted to retreat to helplessness and dependency. Recovering from this state, I discovered that agency exists not only in relation to our external lives, but also to our internal life. Just as I had to stand up and be counted in the world, I had to stand up to the parts of me that tried to suppress other parts.

The team stood up to the aspects of themselves individually and collectively that wanted to stay frozen in impotence and helplessness. As the anaesthetic of excessive dependency wore off, they re-established their agency. Like children accepting that their parents can't provide for them sufficiently, they found alternative ways of getting their needs met: our sessions, regular supervision and a programme of continuing professional development to stimulate and nourish them. Galvanising their resources and identifying realistic sources of care and sustenance gave them hope and impetus. They refound their sense of worth.

Their trust and commitment to the university would take a long time to recover but, as they regained their agency, they recovered their love for the work. They decided that even if they left the service, while they were there, they had to refind their care and compassion for the people the university was meant to be all about – the students.

I worked with the student services team for another eighteen months. Each time they began the insidious descent into basic assumption dependency, someone would exclaim 'muscles!' As if responding to the jolt of an electric rod, they'd shake themselves physically and mentally, and their agency and vitality returned.

They helped me understand that agency isn't the omnipotent belief that we're unaffected by our past and our unconscious, or that mere willpower can determine our lives. Nor is it the view that fate or God determine everything. Agency is knowing that our control is limited and yet, within those limits, taking charge of our lives.

recovered their love for the work. They decided that even if they left the agency, while they were there, they had renewed [illegible] and compassion for the people the agency was [illegible] to be all about—the workers.

[illegible] worked with the treatment [illegible] community. Each time they began [illegible] and adaptation dependency [illegible] would [illegible] to [illegible] in the role of [illegible] themselves physically and mentally [illegible] and ability to continue.

They helped me understand that [illegible] that [illegible] past and [illegible] that [illegible] everything [illegible] that was [illegible] as [illegible] and [illegible] purpose [illegible] of their lives.

16

Illusion

The joyful world of couples dancing in the Renoir print behind her seemed out of reach, almost illusory, in the muted flatness of my meeting with Penny.

Our conversation was part of mediation between Penny and her colleague, Vanessa. They were consultants in an international management consultancy company and, after running an annual event, their relationship was in tatters. Now in its twenty-first year, the event trained leaders and human resources professionals in communication skills. Its worldwide reputation ensured a reliable source of future clients. Although the team had pulled it off, the near failure worried the company. The department instigated mediation to both repair the working relationship between two valued staff members and safeguard the training for the future.

For the last eight years, Penny had been the deputy director of the event. This year the previous director had left, and she'd taken his position. She'd invited Vanessa to be her deputy and together they'd chosen nine colleagues to form the team. The event took place over a long weekend in January 2020; by March, when mediation began, the country was in coronavirus lockdown, so we met on Zoom.

Penny and I got past the usual hiccups: 'Can you hear me?',

'You need to unmute yourself', 'Is your camera on?', before she recounted her unfulfilled dreams for the training, her tone dull, her face cast down.

'I thought I'd be a really good director. Officially, I was the deputy for years, but actually I was the backbone behind the last director. I carried him.'

'Being director yourself wasn't how you'd imagined it?'

She shook her head. 'I thought Vanessa and I would be perfect together. I brought her into the company and mentored her for years. We think alike. We're friends.'

'Friendship can get in the way because you don't want to upset each other.'

'I found that out. It was horrible. I didn't expect to have to pull rank. I wanted us all to work together, with a flat hierarchy and joint decision-making.'

'Flat hierarchies sound good, but we all need clarity about authority.'

'I thought we'd work it out democratically.'

'Democracies still need leaders,' I said.

'I'm so disillusioned.' I heard a sound but couldn't make it out. 'Excuse me,' Penny said. 'I need a drink.' Walking away, the back of her collar slightly askew, she looked fragile and defenceless. She reappeared with a glass of lemonade.

'Vanessa practically accused me of being useless in front of all the staff. She betrayed me.'

Penny's face and shoulders sagged as she explained her hopes to add creativity to the training by reducing the constraints of a rigid structure.

'The previous director always went on about structure and the importance of keeping to the timetable, the plan, the rooms. He was obsessive. I thought structure got in the way and if we were more relaxed there'd be more creativity.'

'What do you mean?'

'Oh, you know, that the participants would come up with innovative ways of improving communication. And staff would too. And we'd be free to play and try things out.'

I couldn't picture Penny playing.

The company claimed to value innovation. Throughout the year, every Wednesday at 10 a.m. they held an innovation and creativity meeting, but creativity didn't oblige by fitting into this schedule. Penny and I agreed that to flourish, creativity needs an environment, rather than a slot. I suspected we had different ideas about what the environment was, but right now I wanted to find out what she felt had gone so wrong with the training and her relationship with Vanessa.

The event had started well, she said, but her attempt to reduce structure hadn't worked because the staff couldn't cope with the freedom. Tensions mounted, stoked by Vanessa complaining until, at the staff meeting on the second day, she'd shouted at Penny.

'She'd turned into a clone of the other director, obsessing about structure, reproaching me for letting the timetable slip, saying no one knew where they were. It was humiliating.'

They'd ended the meeting, got a drink and managed to calm down. With the event in danger of derailing, Penny had taken control. She determined to find a compromise which met both her wish for creativity and Vanessa's for structure. The rest of the staff rejoined them and together they decided to stick to the timetable while adding the use of IT and visual art, to vary communication and stimulate new thinking.

I challenged her notion that stepping in as she had was 'pulling rank'.

'You took charge,' I said. 'It enabled the two of you to get over your row creatively. Perhaps the shouting released the tension and allowed something else.'

'That's kind, but no. All my ideas came to nothing. I should have known they would. Anyhow, it's too late and . . .'

I wondered if her background contributed to the depth of her disillusion. As an only child, Penny told me she'd been used to getting her way. Her parents had tried to have children for many years before she came along. Doting on her, they showered her with gifts: a car for her seventeenth birthday, a small flat when she was twenty-five. They'd paid off library and car parking fines. Until arthritis made it impossible, Penny's mother did her cleaning and ironing.

I felt sure that as a baby and toddler her parents had helpfully encouraged her illusion of omnipotence, quickly appearing when she cried and feeding her as soon as she was hungry. In this way they would have protected her from knowing the world's indifference to her and her powerlessness and dependence on others. But from what she'd said I couldn't imagine them subsequently encouraging her disillusionment; gradually taking a little longer to respond to her demands as she got older, so helping her manage the frustration of waiting. I doubted they gently told her she was too young or not strong enough to do certain things, which would have taught her that while she was cared for and had influence, her power had limits and she was not the centre of everyone's universe.

As Penny talked about her career, it became clear she'd avoided opportunities to shine, yet resented being in the shadows. She'd always, she said, felt undervalued at work. While others got awards and recognition, she remained overlooked.

'Was the training event a chance for your award finally?'

'No. Well, maybe.'

What a trap this pattern must have held her in: disallowing herself the limelight and then stuck with the bitter bile of disappointment.

'That must make this much more painful,' I said.

She nodded at me, the corners of her mouth turning slightly upwards in the smallest of smiles. We talked about what she wanted to say to Vanessa when the three of us met. She hoped to repair their working relationship and also their friendship. I advised her to focus on work; if they got that relationship right perhaps, in time, they could find a way to be friends again. We signed out of our virtual meeting, waving in the slightly ridiculous Zoom way.

I went downstairs and sat on the sofa, feeling disheartened. I was tired from the strain of Zoom, with its millisecond delays and absence of eye contact that reduces our ability to trust and bond with each other. Penny's downcast state had also lowered my mood.

I thought of a coaching client who complained when others got promoted over him, yet always avoided doing the hard work they put in. I suspected I was seeing the same sense of entitlement in Penny. In her case, probably borne from bypassing disillusion as a child. I wondered how she'd coped with the ordinary disillusion of life – the limits of who we are, what we can do and what we're able to achieve.

Although she'd made light of it, I guessed that the pandemic and lockdown contributed to Penny's sense of disillusion. It had taken me some while to understand this aspect of my own loss; that as well as loss from isolation, restriction and fear, I was experiencing loss from disillusionment. As government delayed lockdown, failed to secure adequate personal protective equipment for frontline workers and sent the elderly with Covid back to care homes from hospital, one illusion after another shattered. Disillusion hit me in waves.

Loss through disillusion is opaque and hard to pinpoint, yet its greying hue imprints our mind. And when disillusion overwhelms us, it sears, dragging us down, insidiously gnawing away at hope. In March 2020, I didn't know that worse, far worse, was to come.

The following day I talked to Vanessa. She was working from home alongside homeschooling her seven-year-old son. Near the beginning of our call, he sneaked into the room behind his mum's back and took a quick peek at me on her screen.

Vanessa had thought that being deputy director would be fun and a good opportunity to work with Penny. She was the younger of the two of them and ambitious: she only intended to do the event for a couple of years before moving on to another job.

'I know Penny thought we were friends, but for me we were only ever friendly colleagues.' She said she hoped they'd be able to work together again and forgive each other. I asked what she needed to forgive.

'Mm, that was an odd thing to say wasn't it? I think it's Penny not being a better director. She was my mentor. I idealised her.'

'And at the training event she fell from the pedestal you'd put her on?'

'I suppose she did.'

'And what does Penny need to forgive?' I asked.

'That I showed her up in front of the team.' Vanessa frowned. 'She'd probably say it's also about challenging her, but I think I had to do that rather than let things go wrong.' I agreed that part of the responsibility of a deputy director is, if needs be, to challenge the director in order to protect the event.

'Hello,' I said, seeing her son crawling behind her, trying to be invisible.

He whispered loudly, 'Mummy, Mummy, it's urgent.'

'What are you doing?' she asked, turning towards him.

'I really, *really* need crisps.'

I muffled my laughter. Vanessa narrowed her eyes. 'But you just had . . .' She shook her head. 'OK. Go.'

'Sorry,' she said to me, as he scuttled away.

'It must be hard homeschooling and working at the same time.'

'It's certainly testing my resilience.'

We smiled at the sound of crisps crunching.

'I know I hurt Penny by criticising her in front of the staff, but she'd let everything slip. By the end of the second day, the participants had stopped taking the event seriously. They drifted in and out of sessions, went for coffee whenever they wanted and took extra time for lunch.'

'What did staff do?'

'Nothing. I tried, but Penny harped on about creativity. The training wasn't creative, it was falling apart. Because the participants attendance was erratic and we didn't know what they'd turn up for, staff put little effort into their presentations. And then participants got angry about the lack of content.'

At the lunchtime staff meeting, Vanessa had suggested they adhere to the timetable, but Penny insisted loosening up produced a freedom in which interesting things could happen. They didn't. At the evening staff meeting, Vanessa lost it, shrieking at Penny that structure didn't stop creativity, confusion did.

'Penny screeched back that I was being obsessive like the previous director.' She paused, rubbing her right eye. 'I don't recall much of what we said after that.'

'And the rest of the staff?'

'Watched really. I think they were too shocked to say anything.'

She looked away for a moment. 'I suppose I saw Penny as a bit of a mother-figure.'

'So falling out with her is particularly painful?'

She murmured agreement, looking off camera.

'And maybe it's something to forgive her for?'

'Not being a mother-figure?'

I nodded.

For the first time, Vanessa's face bore something of the pain and disappointment I'd seen in Penny's. Her mother, she told me, had died when she was five years old. Her dad brought her and her brother up with the help of their granny. How crushingly the illusion of parents always being there for her and life being fair must have collapsed. Unlike Penny, disillusion came early for Vanessa – too early and too harshly.

'I don't think I'm capable of illusion,' Vanessa said, when I mentioned this. 'I wish I was. Like I wish I could believe in God. It must be comforting. But I can't.'

As I had with Penny, I talked with Vanessa about what she wanted to say during the joint session, and we said goodbye.

The three of us met the following week. The instant we were all connected, Vanessa looked off camera. Penny sat stiffly, her mouth unsmiling, her face colourless.

'You undermined me,' she accused Vanessa. 'Deliberately undermined me. You made me look stupid. I thought we were friends. I never believed you, of all people, would stab me in the back. Now I realise the signs were there all along. You're selfish. I should never have trusted you.'

I glimpsed tears in Vanessa's eyes, before she lowered her face out of sight.

'I was determined this would be the best training event to date,' Penny continued. 'And I'd be relaxed and responsive as the director, which would enable much more creativity than usual.' She bit her lower lip. 'This was my last chance to finally be number one and show everyone what I can do.'

Vanessa lifted her head again, speaking softly: 'But Penny,

not bothering about structure left us all really anxious. We didn't know where we were with anything. And when problems came up, you didn't want to know. There wasn't a space or time to discuss them.'

'And you thought that saying that in front of the staff would help? You said it was a mess. You made me seem all over the place. A pathetic director.'

'I didn't mean to. Honestly, I didn't. I tried talking to you on your own but you wouldn't listen.'

Vanessa said she would have found it easier if instead of letting the timetable slide, Penny had explained to staff and participants her aim and how the programme would work. Penny wished Vanessa had believed in her and backed her. She certainly hadn't expected her friend to challenge her in public.

Both women looked off camera. After a prolonged silence, Vanessa told Penny she didn't think they were friends. The older woman's eyes widened as if propped open with matchsticks. In one moment, her illusion about a personal and professional relationship had been snatched away.

'Penny, your image froze, can you hear us?' I asked.

'What now?' Vanessa asked as Penny's image vanished. 'Do you think she left deliberately?'

'No, I think it was the line.'

'I don't want to hurt her but what can I say?' Vanessa looked dejected.

The screen flickered and Penny reappeared.

'I'm sorry I keep upsetting you,' Vanessa said. Penny nodded.

I said they had different views and a different investment in the training.

'And in each other,' Penny muttered.

'Yes,' I agreed. 'You both had illusions and were both disillusioned.'

'I can do illusion after all.' Vanessa smiled.

We talked about structure and creativity: the way structure provides the safe environment in which people can play and dream up ideas.

'Abandoning structure was another of my illusions?' Penny asked.

'I think so,' I said.

'I probably wasn't the backbone behind the previous director either,' she muttered.

We all looked drained at the end of our session. It was busy outside, so instead of going for a walk, I listened to music. It seemed the relationship between the two women had broken down when disillusion replaced illusion. The arduous task of reparation was made harder because of the pandemic with its isolation, stress and its own loss of illusions.

At our next individual meeting, Penny told me she felt stupid for romanticising creativity and childishly believing in illusions. I pointed out that illusion had allowed her to finally put herself forward.

Penny snorted. 'Look what happened.'

'Yes, it didn't go brilliantly at first but then you adapted.'

'The disillusionment hurts.'

'About how you ran the event?'

'Yes, and my *friendship* with Vanessa. But mainly about myself.' She dropped her head, as if she could no longer bear its weight.

She'd decided not to direct the event next year. As we talked though, she understood that this would be running away; a return to giving up her agency and hiding in the shadows she'd inhabited for so long. I encouraged her to move forward, develop her directing and leadership skills so she was better equipped to run the event again.

'You think I can?' Penny asked.

'I do.'

'The idea of me repeating it doesn't make you laugh?'

'I don't think you'll simply repeat it. I think you've learnt and will go on learning.'

Penny smiled. A proper, open-mouthed smile.

Vanessa opened our one-to-one Zoom saying she'd realised the irony of the event training in communication skills, and the poor communication between her, Penny and the team.

'If we'd communicated properly, we'd have known how differently we saw things and could have resolved that before the event began.'

Vanessa also recognised that she hadn't taken the role of deputy seriously, more or less going along for the ride and expecting Penny to pull everything together.

'I didn't pull my weight in the run-up. Maybe because of how I saw Penny.'

'An idealised mother-figure, perhaps one that will indulge you?'

'Ouch. Maybe. I was a bit blasé. The event was just a fun thing to do before moving up the ladder, when I'll have to grow up and fun stops.'

'Hopefully not entirely,' I said. But I knew what she meant: while growing up doesn't put an end to fun, it does involve relinquishing many of our illusions and tolerating the ordinary disillusionment of life.

We ended our session and, with both women's decision to run the event again next year, ended the mediation.

I thought of the illusions and disillusions colouring their psychic development, running, sometimes flooding, through their lives. Penny and Vanessa's achievement in the mediation reminded me that emotional maturity, with its keener view of reality, is inexorably tinged by the sorrow and sadness of disillusionment.

17

Difference and Discrimination

Some clients tell me proudly that their organisation 'celebrates difference'. The phrase irritates me. The easy words deny any difficulties. They also stop exploration: if our workplaces and friends declare unambiguous positivity about their diverse workforce, how can individuals own up to less positive feelings? Yet these feelings exist: however good our intentions and benign our beliefs, human beings do not find difference easy. To turn the wish to celebrate from a bland statement into a possibility requires understanding what happens to difference not just in our conscious mind, but in our unconscious.

Our first experience of difference is the pre-verbal, pre-thought awareness that Mum, who at the beginning of life we're inseparable from, isn't an extension of us. She's different; a separate person with her own wants and needs, her own relationships beyond us. We don't have exclusive rights over her. Since our physical and emotional survival depend on her, her difference threatens us. What if someone takes her away or she chooses to leave us?

As we get older, we discover the connection between difference and exclusion. Our first discoveries about our conception tells us that our parents' relationship predates us and we're excluded from some of their activities.

The pain of exclusion imprints our experience of difference. Whether from our parents, our siblings, at school, at work or in our friendship groups, we all experience exclusion to some degree. We learn to better manage the pain it brings, yet at an unconscious level, anything different threatens the mental map of our own small world.

Psychologically, difference also serves our unconscious wish to find receptacles for parts of ourselves and feelings we can't bear. In our minds we split these off and project them into others. It's a flawed solution though as we then see the unwanted parts of ourselves – our brutality for example – in those we project into, and as a result they become frightening to us. By turning these people into 'them' and those we identify with as 'us', we protect one group from our projections and consequent fear, and target another. Those who are 'different' make easy targets – whether the difference is ability/disability, age, class, ethnicity, gender identity, race, religion or sexual orientation.

I'm Jewish and an atheist. My great-grandparents and grandparents were assimilated German, Czech, Austrian and Hungarian Jews. They weren't religious, ate pork, went to synagogue once a year if that, celebrated Christmas and had a Central European culture.

Staunchly German, my maternal great-grandmother refused to leave Berlin. But assimilation meant nothing to the Nazis: she was murdered. Both sets of my grandparents fled with my parents. In Palestine and then Israel, many people shared their background but when they emigrated to the UK with my sister and me years later, my parents found British Jews defined themselves by their religion, or at least their culture. This alienated my parents. If we'd lived in north

London, they might have found belonging easier as there was a community of Central European secular Jewish refugees there. As it was, Mum and Dad kept away from other Jews as they felt they had nothing in common with them. At least, that was the conscious reason. Unconsciously, I think they also believed that in the event of another Holocaust, it was safer to disassociate from other Jews.

Assimilation, secularism, culture, the Holocaust and centuries of antisemitism passed down in their genes and psyches, complicated my family's Jewish identity.

My father talked proudly about Viennese culture and cakes, yet described himself as Czech, never acknowledging his Austrian half. As an old woman, my mother vehemently denied she was German, putting her parentage and the first ten years of her life in Berlin down to 'an accident of birth'.

Dad feared people knowing he was Jewish. When, for example, his bank manager recommended an accountant, adding, 'I hope you don't mind that he's Jewish,' Dad didn't say anything.

Dad's sister, my aunt, came to England on her own in 1938. She was seventeen and too old to go on the family ticket to Palestine. While England provided physical safety, it didn't provide freedom from antisemitism and – terrified of persecution – in 1944, my aunt, her cousins and uncle were baptised. Perhaps unconsciously, baptism also signified their shame: the stain of shame among Jews. 'Like lambs to the slaughter', Jews say about concentration camp victims. They call up this shame when extolling 'Never again', a phrase commonly used by some Israeli politicians.

Many persecuted groups experience such shame. A black member of a team I consulted to talked about the shame and anguish of having allowed herself to be subjugated.

Shame can turn to anger and accusation: Jews insult each

other with the phrase 'self-hating Jews'. It's mainly used against those critical of the state of Israel. The conflation of opposition to the state with antisemitism is, in my view, political. Yet, underneath that, the phrase attests to the inevitable internalisation that occurs in Jews, as in all groups at the receiving end of ongoing racism.

In my parents this created contradictions. With olive skin and dark hair, Mum reacted to Hitler's notion of Aryans as blonde and blue-eyed by disliking blondeness and ascribing beauty to darkness – the darker the better. She'd tan with great dedication, proud of how brown she could go. Yet she had a fair husband and two fair children. The contradiction didn't pose a problem for her but confused me.

I always wanted a tan too, yet when I was the only white staff member in a workshop in India, a country that uses large quantities of skin whitening products, I found myself liking my colour in a way I never had before or have since. Such is the power of unconscious projections.

My father acquired his mother's snobbishness. She saw herself as Viennese – a cut above other Austrians. I think the snobbery, combined with the inferiority Dad internalised as a Jew, inverted in his unconscious and became superiority. He looked down at anything or anyone he deemed lacking in intellect or culture. Projecting into them his sense of inadequacy probably covered up and defended against the inferiority he found intolerable.

Growing up I thought of my Jewishness like my gender: an unquestioned, fundamental part of my identity. On the surface, it played little part in my life. As a teenager, I chose not to attend school assembly on the grounds of atheism, not Judaism. On the rare occasions I experienced direct antisemitism, it shocked me. At university it didn't occur to me that my consistently low marks from one tutor might relate to my background, until another tutor pointed this out. And when, having disagreed about the tip for bad service in a restaurant, a friend told me not to be 'Jewish', I was stunned.

The complexity of embodying both victim and persecutor as both Jewish and German, only struck me in my early forties. I wondered why it had passed me by for so long. Years later, I understood; I'd imbibed my parents' method of dealing with it through splitting and denial. It only dawned on me while writing this chapter that the powerful narrative of my father being only Czech stopped me seeing that the presence of both victim and persecutor came from my father as well as my mother. I'm not only a German Jew, but also, in part, an Austrian Jew – something I still find hard to acknowledge.

In psychoanalysis, I found that the outer reality had inscribed itself as an inner reality and a victim/persecutor dynamic operated in my mind. I didn't live through the Holocaust, but it lived through me in this mirror of my mixed heritage and my family's persecution. Claiming my own identity, rather than simply being a product of my family's history, entailed understanding the effect of persecution and consequent confusion in the family. It meant examining what I had imbibed and my own internal Jewishness.

I think this process of disentangling ourselves and our identity – as much as that's possible – is true for all of those coming from a group that's experienced the impact of long-term prejudice and discrimination.

For me, the disentangling also involved other Jews who frequently tried to meld me to their versions of my identity. In 2005, I participated in a five-day experiential workshop in Israel about Jewish identity and the diaspora. The welcome from my fellow Jews moved me until I understood the price tag. My birthplace, Jerusalem, held special meaning for them (as it did for me) and seemed to inflate their wish to bring me into the fold. Or, in their eyes, bring me *back* into the fold. The rabbi among the participants took it on himself to teach me about Judaism; the others tightened their grip around me. It seemed the only way to join them was to hide who I was and submit to the group. Knowing I wouldn't or couldn't do this pained me.

At one point, I found myself in a small group with an orthodox 'settler' living in a newly formed town built on land which – in the eyes of the world – Israel illegally occupied and – in the eyes of some of the orthodox – was their rightful place. She stood for everything I opposed. We were opposites in beliefs, culture and way of life as well as politics. Yet, we managed to articulate this and see each other as real people rather than as stereotypes. We didn't change our political views, but we enjoyed working well together and creating constructive action in the workshop. This helped me to find a tentative place in the wider group, that didn't involve either submerging or excluding myself.

Recently a Jewish friend repeated an argument I've heard countless times: she insisted being Jewish was a religion, not an ethnicity. When I said I wasn't religious, she qualified the definition: Jewishness is a culture. 'Not for me,' I said. She tried again: 'If Hitler would categorise you as Jewish, you're Jewish.'

That's it? My ethnicity defined by nothing but racism? My mother wondered this too. She came to believe that our family wouldn't be Jewish if it wasn't for Hitler. I disagreed, though at the time couldn't articulate a more positive identity. Now I've concluded that my Jewish identity relates to my ethnicity and origins. It's the history of my family and the particular way that part of my background shapes me.

In the workplace, my Jewish identity had little place or relevance. I didn't think of the crude antisemitism I faced in my first job as anything to do with my experience of work. I was a nursing assistant in an adolescent unit for mentally ill boys. One of them sent me an anonymous note made from letters cut out from newspapers. It was a death threat, telling me that as a 'stinking Jew' my days were numbered. My memory is hazy now, but I think he made a grotesque reference to a Nazi atrocity – skin or lampshades. I never knew how he found out my ethnicity, but I understood that in his illness, it provided a hook for his hatred. The staff reassured me it wasn't personal; he'd always hated Jews. Their comments helped in a way, yet also made it harder as I felt unable to express my very personal feelings and fear.

Because this came from a patient, I dismissed it. Yet, my dismissal ignored a distressing fact: that I can so easily become one of those 'others', the 'them' who receives the hatred and projections from the 'we'. In my blindness to this, I also missed seeing how I did the same thing to other people. My disdain to the orthodox among the Jews and other religions; and, at times, my superiority towards people of colour.

My first experience of my colour-based racism occurred during a study-visit to Ghana in 1979. My initial surprise at seeing black people running the banks, the schools, everything, shook me. In the UK, I'd never seen black people in such positions. But it was more than that; part of my surprise came from the recognition that this possibility hadn't occurred to me.

Colour doesn't feature in antisemitism, yet its pernicious presence commonly forms part of the hierarchy of Jews. In Israel the Central European Ashkenazy Jews retain the highest status, while the darker Sephardi Jews face more discrimination and African Jews sit at the bottom of the pile.

My ancestors weren't persecuted because of the colour of their skin. Neither were they owned. No one insured them as cargo on freight ships and claimed compensation for lost goods if they died or were thrown overboard. Ghana opened my eyes to slavery; I imagine it gives rise to particular constellations in the mind.

After the trip to Ghana, I started teaching in a further education college in Birmingham. I was working with unemployed young people in 1981 during what became known as the Brixton, Handsworth and Toxteth riots that spread across London, Birmingham, Liverpool, Leeds and Manchester, as well as other cities. Under the Thatcher government unemployment rocketed, hitting Birmingham's West Indian community hard; frustration grew as racism and youth unemployment denied black youngsters opportunities. The police arrested some of my black students who happened to be in the wrong place at the wrong time. One, despite his innocence, served time. I'd never seen the reality of colour-based racism and its discrimination and injustice close up before.

As my career progressed, my world became increasingly middle class and white. I missed working with young people, yet looking back it also brought comfort. No longer witnessing the effects of daily racism on black students removed my distress and rage, as well as my shame. I knew that I wouldn't have been arrested for walking down the street in Handsworth at the time of the riots. I knew I had opportunities not afforded to the working class or people of colour, and especially not to those in both categories. They couldn't escape, but I could. And distance from their lives was easier.

Not long after the start of the civil war in Syria, when we heard daily about president Bashar Al-Assad's appalling treatment of his own people, I directed a three-day experiential workshop about leadership and followership for students in a university. At the end of the first day, we held a large group event, with the task of exploring what was happening in the here and now of the group both consciously and unconsciously. As usual in such events, the only structure was the strict adherence by staff to starting and ending on time, working to the task, and maintaining our role. Three of us consulted to the large group: me, a white man and a black man. A moment before it finished, one of the students, who'd been glaring at me for much of the session, said, 'If you staff believe this is a good way of learning, you're worse than Assad.' He turned his eyes from me to my black colleague, his words slow and deliberate. 'And you, you're a fucking cunt.' A black student stood up and shouted at him to shut up; another black student walked out. For the remaining seconds of the session, we, the staff, sat paralysed in horror.

At the start of the next day, I opened the short review meeting for all staff and participants by saying that what had happened and what was said to Omari (the black staff member) was unacceptable. Relief passed around the room. The student concerned sat in silence. Someone asked what we'd do if something like this happened again. I said the person would have to leave. Some students nodded saying they'd been so upset they'd almost left the workshop.

I felt relief too, especially since some staff hadn't wanted me to say anything or name the black staff member. I was glad I'd stuck to my instinct but still question my silence in the few seconds before the session ended. I'm grateful to the student who spoke up and to the other one for leaving the room. I wish I'd found my voice as a white person as well as the director, instead of leaving it to black students.

It's easy to see this shocking event as a one-off. Yet, a moment before abusing the black staff member, the student had been hostile towards me as the director. I think this sudden redirection came from deeply ingrained systemic racism.

Systemic discrimination, the journalist and sociologist Professor Gary Younge says, isn't 'isolated incidents, but a range of processes built on presumption, assumption, confidence, ignorance and exclusory institutional, personal and professional networks all buttressed by the dead weight of privilege'.

The disproportionate effect of Covid-19 on people of colour demonstrated the devastating effect of this. Younge pointed out that NHS employers are far more likely to refer black and Asian doctors to the General Medical Council for fitness to practice than their white colleagues, leading to investigations that can finish, or certainly damage, their careers. While many in this group feel bullied or harassed, the fear of recrimination frequently stops them speaking out. Another group, migrant health workers, faced immigration insecurity during Covid, unsure about the renewal of their visas after Brexit. They were also the group most frequently on zero-hour contracts. Legitimised by Brexit, racism towards all 'foreigners' rose significantly after the referendum in 2016, surging even further during the pandemic. In this context, migrant health workers or people of colour were likely to be 'less insistent in demanding personal protective equipment (PPE)' than their white colleagues and so more exposed to Covid-19.

Although racism occurs whatever our colour, the legacy of colonisation and slavery, and the perpetuation of vast inequality in wealth and power that, in the main, favours white people, is unparalleled. The centuries old continuing narrative and projections of white superiority have become embedded in our psyches. Even when we consciously break these, they linger in our unconscious.

Over the years, I accepted that as a white person in a racist society, my own racism was inevitable. It took me longer to see the defensiveness in that truism. Like the declaration about celebrating difference, it closed down exploration and circumvented change.

Exploration meant recognising what my privilege caused and appreciating that I have to go to the back of some queues in order to contribute to a rebalance. But change requires action, not just exploration. I've made small changes in my everyday life and work. I've opened up spaces for clients of colour to talk about their experience – not the one they or others think they ought to have but the one they do have with all its complexity.

In a team in a university, for instance, I created a space for the one black staff member to talk about his experience in the otherwise all-white department. It was June 2020: we'd recently witnessed the murder of George Floyd on our TV screens and smart devices and white people finally began to see what people of colour live with. A discussion followed and led to the team producing a statement about Black Lives Matter for all students.

After I'd referred to the Black Lives Matter movement twice in a consultation to another team, a black member picked it up. They never, she said, talked about race, even though some of the team and a number of their clients were black or brown. A painful, yet vital conversation had at least begun.

While I've always paid attention to all differences, I became more deliberate about instigating conversations about their impact on staff and stakeholders in organisations. I tried to ensure minority experiences weren't drowned out by the majority or that the issues hardest to talk about weren't lost in a generalised conversation.

Some differences are easier to talk about than others. I found talking about my early experiences of overt sexism and sexual harassment when I first entered the workforce much easier than talking about being Jewish. Recently I worked with a team who had no problem discussing their cultural differences; the more difficult issue was for those new to the sector to talk about their professional difference.

Talking about difference in the workplace isn't about false celebrations. It's about the optimism and hope of staying with the difficulties of seeing each other and working together with our differences; something akin to my encounter with the orthodox settler in the Israeli workshop. To do that, we have to first examine ourselves and notice our discomforts, so we can better tolerate the pain of exclusion and keep hold of more of those aspects of ourselves we'd like to disown.

When we turn people into the other, the 'them' we feel superior to and dump with our least attractive qualities, we dehumanise ourselves as well as the victims of our prejudice. Because we deny reality and deceive ourselves. We give in to our destructiveness and lose our capacity for love and compassion, for empathy and decency.

I don't underestimate the challenge of changing this. As with all change, it involves loss. Loss of who and what we thought we were as a country and loss of privilege. Giving up some of our advantages as white people requires commitment to justice and equality. It requires courage to face the truth of our individual and collective past. And it takes courage for all of us to risk the response when we say what we think or feel.

Whatever our fears, we can only progress towards more humane workplaces – and a more humane society – by tackling difference and discrimination. Without understanding what happens in our minds, celebrations of difference will continue to be hollow, and the splitting and projection, the distress and rage and violence will persist. Alternatively, with understanding and continual work that's often tough and demanding, we can use the kaleidoscope of our different approaches to work and thinking, and our different colours, backgrounds, cultures and identities in creative and generative ways.

PART THREE

FINDING OURSELVES

18

Changing Patterns

The patterns our unconscious sets during our childhood become part of our personality: our attachment patterns, our defences, the way we relate to others and to ourselves. Patterns also become imprinted by the scripts handed to us by parents and teachers: the good girl, the lazy one, the clever one, the one that soaks up the tension in the family or looks after a parent, the one that makes everyone laugh. Once set, patterns are hard to shift.

As in our personalities, patterns are set in our organisations and become part of organisational culture. We unknowingly imbibe both good and bad patterns. The negative ones repeat themselves, causing us problems both individually and in the workplace.

This 'repetition compulsion', as we saw earlier, results from repressing experiences or feelings we find too difficult to process. We push them into our unconscious, hoping they will go away. Instead, we repeat them, sometimes in another guise.

Repetition compulsion replaces thoughtful remembering with unthinking, recurrent actions. It keeps us locked in a state of stasis. Noticing these repetitions gave us no pleasure led Freud to the notion of the death instinct or death drive – a dulling force exerting us away from life to inertia.

But what if there is another repetition? One that is on the side of life rather than against it?

I first had this idea in 2008 when I heard Daniel Barenboim playing the thirty-two Beethoven Piano Sonatas in eight concerts over three weeks at London's Royal Festival Hall. I had never been to so many concerts in such a short space of time, or listened to the complete cycle of sonatas, composed by Beethoven over the course of almost thirty years. The music, and Barenboim's virtuoso performances, transported me to other worlds, while concurrently taking me deep within my internal world.

Barenboim also gave two talks; at one of these I asked him his thoughts about music as a source of integration. I explained that for me he symbolised both internal and external integration. Internally, his expression and mobility as a pianist, moving so fluidly between every emotion, suggested an integrated mind. He seemed aware of different and 'other', seemingly foreign, parts of himself and of the actual 'other' – the person or race that is different from us. Externally, he grew up in Israel and his partnership with the Palestinian Edward Said and their West–Eastern Divan Orchestra, represented a positive and hopeful external integration in an area suffused with disintegration and destructiveness.

Barenboim beamed. I wouldn't know this he said, but his latest book, just out in the US was called *Everything is Connected: The Power of Music.* He answered my question enthusiastically; some of what he said was lost on me as I'm not musically trained, but the word 'accumulation' struck me, as did 'repetition', which he mentioned later. I didn't know what he meant but, with his words in my mind, I listened keenly, and somehow differently, at the next concert. As the beauty and humanity of Beethoven washed over me, I heard something new. That is when I had the idea of developmental repetition sitting alongside Freud's repetition compulsion.

This positive repetition can be glimpsed in the moments of repetition compulsion when we attempt to conquer something psychically that we previously found impossible. Although we remain stuck in the gossamer of repetition compulsion, such moments are accompanied by hope. And hope indicates the possibility of another kind of repetition.

I am calling this 'repetition progression'. It emanates from and is an ally of our life drive, which animates rather than dissipates life. If our drive towards death overshadows our drive for life it cannot exist.

This is the repetition that commonly exists in classical music. A sequence of notes reappears, yet the music changes. The original notes might be joined by other notes, a different key or rhythms and dynamics. The context has changed. Through this repetition and accumulation, a different sound is made, the expression alters. Our emotional response shifts and we gain a new perspective. The repetition and accumulation are dynamic, bringing about progression and change.

The words of Dr Kadiatu Kanneh, at a musical tribute by the cellist Sheku Kanneh-Mason and his family to George Floyd, following his murder on 25 May 2020, resonate with this:

'Music is a testament to suffering, to hope and to love. Let it be a testament to change.'

Music describes and evokes our deepest emotions and existential questions. Because they are contained and transmitted through the music, we can access feelings and parts of ourselves we might otherwise shut out.

So, whereas repetition compulsion is destructive and stuck, repetition progression is mobile and transformative. The conscious use of repetition in music, both in form and content, enters our unconscious, enabling us to deviate from our previous knowledge and assumptions. Dislocated and relocated, we become open to something new.

The second movement of Beethoven's *Waldstein* sonata illustrates this. It starts slowly and hesitantly. A basic melody – a sequence of notes – is repeated regularly. The slowness, pauses and space between notes present us with the relationship between sound and silence. But this changes; different notes, dynamics and tempo join the original sequence of notes. The pauses go, the hesitancy changes to confidence. Difficulties have been overcome and the music flows proud, joyous and triumphant. The repetitious structure attunes our ears and we feel safe. Like a baby in our mother's arms, our anxiety subsides. We know this place. The security opens a space for our curiosity. The familiar allows us to take in the unfamiliar. We can let go of our existing knowledge and assumptions and open up to a change in direction, new emotions, experiences and understanding.

The *Waldstein* illustrates how repetition progression integrates different parts. Similarly, psychoanalysis can integrate different parts of our personality. Our destructive or unwanted parts do not go away but other tones and notes are added and, as in music, where one element once dominated, another comes into focus. The chords and sound of our personality develop and shift.

Repetition progression can also take place where our different parts remain unintegrated and irreconciled to each other. When our greed and generosity, for instance, cannot get along together but have to coexist. In our minds, this is managed by the ego. In music, it is managed firstly by the composer and then by the conductor and musicians.

In Beethoven's final piano sonata (no. 32, Op. 111), the music erupts from the silence preceding it. To me, the opening conjures up death and rage about its inevitability. We are caught in an almost impossible tension; it's unbearable to stay with the emotion, and unbearable to turn away. And then the tension is released and suddenly we find ourselves in a completely different vista – open, expansive, sublime.

The essence and power of the first movement is its fragmentation. The falling apart, disintegration bound within the structure and shape of the repetition in the music, holds us enough so we can get lost. We do not have any idea where we are, or where we are going. Through the dislocation we absorb the added layers and progression into a dramatic change in emotion and direction. Now we hear previously unimagined futures. The different parts coexist rather than integrate.

Music, Barenboim says, always has opposing elements coexisting together. In their independent voices we hear and distinguish between both oppositional and unifying aspects. Each has its own special moment or moments. The diverse stories and identities sit side by side, with acceptance and conflict, with tension, contradiction, sometimes harmony, sometimes discord.

In an orchestra, every musician and every instrument have their individual place and identity. But their existence is within, and dependent on, the group. If one player fails to hear others, it does not work. If they cannot manage their own part or restrain their need to either shine or hide, it does not work. If a trumpet plays too loudly, a flute cannot be heard. If the orchestra does not concede to the music, the personality of the music cannot be heard.

Coexistence is fundamental to the West–Eastern Divan Orchestra, the organisation set up in 1999 by Daniel Barenboim and Edward Said. They initially undertook to hold a summer workshop for young musicians from Israel and the Arab countries 'to promote coexistence and intercultural dialogue', but soon created a full orchestra. They met in Germany and the first players were Palestinian (from within Israel, the occupied territories and other Arab countries where they lived as refugees), Egyptian, Jordanian, Lebanese, Syrian and Israeli. There were also a few German players. Today, the orchestra's home is in Spain. An equal number of Arab and Israeli musicians form the base of the orchestra, along with players from Turkey, Iran and Spain. They get together for rehearsals and an international concert tour each summer.

After Said died in 2003, Barenboim continued to develop music-based projects in the occupied territories. The partnership was maintained by Said's widow, Mariam. The Barenboim–Said Foundation, Ramallah, Palestine, began in 2003 and in 2005, the West–Eastern Divan played a landmark concert there. Doing this involved considerable risks: it was and still is illegal for Israelis to go into the Palestinian territories; it was and still is illegal for Syrians and Lebanese citizens to go to Israel, which they had to do in order to get to Ramallah.

The only thing the musicians agree on is that there is no military solution to the Israeli–Palestinian conflict. Other than that, there is no single opinion; the tensions and differences are expected and accepted. Barenboim and Said's partnership reaches across the divided states and peoples. They can be seen as a parental couple who gave birth to and nurture the orchestra.

Barenboim and Said's book, *Parallels and Paradoxes*, illustrates the significant moments of repetition progression in the privacy of the workshop where Israelis see that Arabs can play classical music and Arabs open their informal Arabic music improvisation sessions to Israelis. Repetition progression exists in the act of making music together within this joint Semitic dialogue where noise is converted to sound. It is there in the members of the orchestra, Arabs and Jews, sharing territory, in the discipline of learning and rehearsing music and in repeating individual and collective stories.

It is not just the identity of the music that is expressed and developed, but the identity of these young musicians. And it is not just music that is heard and listened to, but Arab and Israeli narratives. Players report staying up until the early hours of the morning talking to each other, and hearing, often for the first time, the experiences of the 'other'. Sometimes it is not the other we might expect; a Palestinian musician from Israel commented during an interview for the 2008 Proms that he knows Israelis (both Jews and Palestinians); the people he did not know and had no means of contact with until joining the orchestra, were other Palestinians. He had no sense of his own people other than those living under occupation.

Barenboim, who in 2008 became the only person to hold both Israeli and Palestinian citizenship, believes passionately in the importance of narrative. The two sides do not have to agree with one another, but they have to hear each other. He talks about the need for 'sensitive speaking and painful listening'. Many of the musicians, he says, 'hear the pain of the other side's narrative for the first time during the workshop, and this is inevitably a shock that also requires them to think about the past, and about the suffering that has continued over so many years'.

As they face reality and mourn, I imagine the repetitious structure and discipline of rehearsals, along with the emotional resonance in the music they play and the Israeli–Palestinian parental couple, provide emotional containment. This allows highly charged, complex emotions – including grief and conflict – to discharge safely in a way that progresses understanding and coexistence.

As repetition progression helped this organisation, it can

help others entrenched in the destructive patterns of repetition compulsion. In one company I worked with, the same issues wreaked havoc for years. I'd run several workshops where they'd rehearsed their old wounds and disagreements. I thought we were making progress when, in our last workshop, the assistant chief executive turned to the chief executive and said it was all down to him. He was the cause of all their problems, she couldn't work with him and didn't like him. She turned to me and asked if this was supposed to happen at the end of working with me. 'No,' I said, desperately trying to think what to do next. I thought it was a disaster, but I was wrong. I hadn't seen that after going over and over the same ground, they had veered off onto a new path. The new place looked as if it was filled with destructiveness, but it allowed them to venture into a space where they could have different, more open conversations and gain new understanding. To my amazement, it was the beginning of their recovery.

This team showed me the importance of creating opportunities that enable a shift towards repetition progression by instigating ongoing, regular dialogue and reflection, where we learn to listen to each other's stories and experiences. This kind of talking and listening moves beyond the old scripts based on preconceptions that confirm our views and reinforce our stuck patterns and polarised positions. Instead, it encourages the repetition of our scripts to become the repetition progression of our stories. Stories with a historical, rather than mythical past, a co-authored present and as yet unknown, but jointly shaped future. Talking and listening where our curiosity, rather than our defences, flourish and we accumulate fresh ideas and understanding.

19

Love Refound

'I was scared I'd cry if we met in private,' Sebastian said. He was the managing director of a literary agency, and we were in the coffee bar of a museum in central London. We'd originally arranged to meet nearby in a room they used opposite the agency, but the night before Sebastian had emailed asking to move it here. I'd almost said no, we needed a private space, but I realised his request must have meaning, so agreed.

We sat at a small wooden table furthest away from the long stainless steel counter faced by bar stools. The low hum of chatter and the soft clanking of cups filled the space.

A tall man, in smart black jeans, black shirt and a cream linen jacket, Sebastian regarded me with piercing eyes. I guessed he was in his late thirties. The agency, founded by him, Emilia and Ben, had just celebrated its eighth anniversary. They'd begun with five authors but now represented more than two hundred and fifty across a wide range of genres.

They'd asked me for help as after the first couple of years, tension and friction broke out between them, rising and ebbing but never going away. Recently it had blown up again and was affecting morale throughout the agency.

'It's tearing us apart,' Sebastian said. 'I feel so betrayed by Ben and Emilia.' He explained that although they were brilliant agents, they didn't take their management responsibilities as directors seriously.

'It's not just about our own clients, our own work, it's about supporting the other agents and leading the work of the whole agency.'

For example, Ben always inducted new staff but had done this so half-heartedly for the last two hires, Sebastian had had to take over. And Emilia was meant to keep the website up to date but hadn't and again Sebastian had to step in. Everything, Sebastian complained, landed unfairly with him.

The sound of raucous laughter from the three young women perched on stools at the counter interrupted us.

'I can't remember the last time Emilia, Ben and I laughed like that,' Sebastian said. 'We had such fun in the early days.' He shook his head.

When he talked about his children and wife, Sebastian beamed with pride.

'It's not just me; the way I work is unfair on them. The kids are young. They need me. My wife needs me but I'm at the office all hours. Emilia keeps disappearing – I don't know why – so I can't even ask her to step in on some things.'

Before I could ask about Emilia's disappearances, he continued, telling me how important family has always been to him. His dad, retired now, was headmaster of a public school; Mum was a librarian. His sister is a successful playwright. They're a close family, with a strong work ethic and sense of right and wrong.

'Perhaps the agency felt like family at the beginning,' I ventured.

'It really did. In a way it still does.'

'But now it's a dysfunctional one?'

'Exactly.' He looked around. 'Those lights are new,' he said, pointing to the low hanging brass lights over the coffee counter.

He turned back to me. 'I'm thinking of leaving. I don't know how much more I can take. I've put everything into the agency so I really don't want to go, but I think it would be best if I cut my losses, sold my shares and started up on my own.'

'That would be momentous.'

He nodded. 'I love the agency. I love the work. I love the guys. Well, I used to . . .' He looked around again as though summoning help from the room. 'I don't know what else I can do except leave and start again.'

Emilia and Ben had texted to let me know they'd also meet me in the museum coffee bar. Ben came fifteen minutes after Sebastian left. He got himself a cappuccino.

'Seb's brilliant. He's the inspiration and business head behind our success. But he's impossible.'

Stretching his legs out to the side of the table, he complained that Sebastian didn't listen. The latest fallout was over joining up with another agency.

'Emilia and I were very unsure. We suspected they may be out to take us over, rather than join us. We wanted to find out more, think it through. But it turns out Seb was already cosying up to the two founders there – lunches, drinks, dinner – and the next thing, despite us saying to find out more, he'd already started negotiating with them. How dare he? He doesn't take us seriously.'

Between sips of cappuccino, Ben talked about the close friendship between the three of them in the early years. It had faded until it was extinct. He couldn't remember the last time they'd met socially.

'I'm forty. My dad was sixty when he died. Who knows how long I've got? My partner and I want to live abroad for a bit. I haven't told Seb and Emilia yet. We want to go in the next few years and before that reduce our working hours, so we enjoy life more.' He talked enthusiastically about wanting more time for simple things like going to exhibitions and away for weekends. And reading – not just for work but for pleasure.

'For now, I'm establishing boundaries. I said no, for example, when Seb asked me to redo the way we log submissions, because I'd have to do it out of hours, alongside all my reading in the evenings and at the weekend. I know it pissed Seb off but that's too bad.'

A man who looked vaguely familiar came up and greeted him enthusiastically. 'One of my authors,' Ben explained when he'd gone. 'One of our first actually. Unknown then. A household name now.' His face and tone, even his bearing, became livelier as he told me about the early heady days of the agency.

'Work is so tiring now.' His voice dropped. 'I'm still committed to what we do but I'm sick of the arguments and tension. And of being treated like a junior director and marginalised. It's as much my company as Seb's for God's sake.' He put his cup down slowly. 'I'm thinking of leaving.'

I went to the toilet and returned to the same table, feeling tense and weighed down. When Emilia arrived, the surrounding tables had filled with people having afternoon tea. We found a quiet spot in a side room off the main café.

'Seb is brilliant but impossible,' she said, the same words Ben had used. The disagreements between the three of them used to blow over quickly, but gradually the bad feeling stayed. The quarrel about joining up with the other agency was huge, but sometimes small things blew up out of all proportion. Like who they used to print their rights guides or which firm sent out books. The row would end, but the feeling hung around like a bad taste.

'I'm not sure if . . .' She hesitated, before asking if I wanted another coffee.

'I'm getting one,' she said when I looked unsure. I asked for mint tea. I watched her go to the coffee bar, wondering why she'd interrupted herself.

'My dad's in hospital,' she said when she came back with our drinks. 'Again. He's always suffered from acute anxiety.'

She hadn't told anyone at work.

'Seb and Ben treat me as a bit dippy and volatile as it is. I'm rather scatter-brained. And sometimes I lose my temper. I don't want them thinking I'm unstable too. Like my dad.' She tucked one hand under her leg.

Emilia told me her parents hadn't taken her going into agenting well. They'd always wanted her to become a doctor, lawyer or architect. A 'proper' job with security and prospects. Agenting didn't cut it for them; her refusal to change careers and their constant nagging caused a rift. She was in regular contact with her parents and brother at the moment, but only because of the situation with her dad; usually, she saw little of them.

We finished our drinks. As we were about to go Emilia drew breath. She tied and retied the silk scarf around her neck. My shoulders and neck stiffened. Not all three of them surely.

'I haven't made a final decision, but I may leave.'

On the tube home, I replayed the three conversations. None of them knew that they were all contemplating leaving, yet it seemed a real possibility. I felt loaded with their secrets.

In the morning I waited at reception in the agency as we'd agreed. An impressive display of their authors' books covered the wall behind the receptionist. Sebastian, Emilia and Ben arrived fifteen minutes late. We headed across the road to the office space where they rented a room. Three black squashy sofas, each scattered with soft cushions in swirls of purple and green, dominated the space. A glass coffee table stood in the middle. Prints of abstract art got lost on the large expanse of white walls. If you looked up, the atmosphere suggested a picture from a magazine – soulless and without people to mess it up. If you looked at the sofas and cushions, it conjured up a boudoir.

Sebastian sat opposite me; Emilia and Ben occupied the two ends of the middle sofa. I wanted to remind them of when they'd worked well together, so asked them what they liked and admired about each other. My request surprised them but was fruitful; the tension visibly eased as they remembered what they valued in each another. Sebastian's inspirational vision and business focus, Ben's ability to draw in the big names, Emilia's unfailing knack to foresee trends. The incredible drive and commitment, including the financial investment, they'd each put in to establishing the agency. The fun and pride of taking on unknown authors and helping establish them, as well as taking on those who'd already made it and wanted to move to a more dynamic agency, the kick of being among the premier agencies in the UK with close connections to some fantastic agencies in the US.

'Remember when Ben signed Antonio? And we got six-figure deals on both sides of the Atlantic, and a film option all on the same day!' They laughed, recalling the copious amount of champagne they drank that evening. And the wine fridge Seb ordered that arrived the next day ready stocked with champagne for future big deals.

'And then straight into our first Frankfurt Book Fair. When publishers who didn't know us were coming to our table trying to pre-empt Antonio's book for their country, offering over the odds to get the deal done and off the table.'

'Everyone was asking who we were.'

I moved on to the difficulties that had to be aired if they were to stand a chance of repairing their relationships and rebuilding the agency's foundation after almost a decade of feuding. I asked them to write the issues from the past that were still affecting them on Post-its.

'All of the issues?' Emilia asked. I nodded.

'Are you sure?'

'Yes.'

'All of them?' she repeated when I asked them to put their Post-its on the wall.

'Yes.' I held my breath.

The most difficult theme they said, as we read the Post-its, was the divide between Seb and the other two. Ben looked at Sebastian apologetically. 'You won't want to hear this, but I feel pushed out and marginalised. Sorry.'

Emilia nodded. 'Me too. And excluded.'

Sebastian glanced at me. I gave a slight nod of my head.

He looked at his business partners. 'I don't think you have a clue how I feel in all this. You say you're marginalised and excluded but I feel abandoned. Abandoned and betrayed.'

He talked about the things they'd dumped with him. How he couldn't even find Emilia some of the time and Ben refused work that meant he had to do it. They responded with accusations about the other agency – how despite knowing they weren't happy, Seb had gone ahead and started negotiating.

'I was waiting for that. I knew you'd swipe me with it,' Seb said, his voice bitter.

'It has to be talked about, but let's first try to understand how the three of you have got to this place,' I said.

They nodded glumly. I continued, suggesting that Sebastian's large, charismatic personality could make it difficult for Emilia and Ben to find their place. Equally, their withdrawal pushed Sebastian into filling up more of the space.

Ben said it came naturally for him to slip off to a place on the margins as he had as a teenager, knowing he was gay and not daring to come out. Emilia recalled withdrawing as a child from the fights between her parents and older brother.

'I'd spend hours alone in my room reading or drawing. Anything to keep away from the tensions.'

'You started this agency together,' I said. 'You both need to step forward again and, Sebastian, you need to make space for them.'

'It's not that easy,' Emilia said.

'I know, but that's why we're here isn't it?' I asked. They nodded, a mix of hope and despair on their faces.

'Seb doesn't even have time for us now anyway,' Ben said. He turned to look at the other man. 'You go for lunch and drinks with those two directors from the other agency but not with us.'

'And we're the other directors, your business partners, in *this* agency,' Emilia added.

Seb protested before begrudgingly admitting he preferred the company of the directors in the other agency.

'You're creating the wrong threesome. Seb and the founders from the other agency, instead of you three,' I said. They looked baffled.

'You three are the founders. Sebastian's threesome with the two other founders reinforces Emilia and Ben's positions at the margins instead of at the centre,' I explained.

We stopped for a break. I stayed in the room; they went across the road to the agency. Sebastian returned first. When Emilia and Ben came back and sat down again, the three of them drew breath in unison. They laughed. This must have been what they were like in the early days, I thought; minutely attuned to one another.

'I suppose I turned to the other agency because I couldn't stand the friction between us,' Seb acknowledged.

'It's been hard watching that. I was jealous, to be honest,' Ben said.

'It's our agency,' Emilia said.

'Yes, but where are you?' Sebastian replied.

At the end of the session they agreed to avoid any difficult conversations until the next time we met. They were too fragile to risk airing issues on their own yet.

The following week, they arrived late again. I thought it might be an expression of their ambivalence about the sessions but opted not to say anything; I didn't want to risk them feeling told off as we began.

I asked them how they were. 'Fine.' 'All right.'

'How are you really?' I asked.

'Fine.'

'Do you ask each other this?'

'It's intrusive,' Seb said, taking the lid on and off his pen, 'We don't do that.'

'You need to. It's not about intruding into each other's private lives. You're partners. You need to know enough so that you can work well together and manage the agency. You need to know, for example, if something is going on with one of you, so you can respond and cover for one another if needs be.'

Sebastian took the pen lid on and off faster. 'My mum has dementia.'

'What?' Emilia said. 'I didn't have a clue.'

'I'm so sorry,' Ben said.

'You didn't know either?' I asked. He shook his head.

A plane flying overhead cast a shadow across the room.

'I'm really sorry, Sebastian,' I said. He nodded, saying that, as Emilia and Ben knew, she'd had cancer before but was given the all-clear a few months ago. Then last month came this diagnosis.

'Oh my God,' Emilia muttered.

'That's so bloody unfair,' Ben said.

At lunchtime, I went to the coffee bar in the museum and prepared for the afternoon as I munched my way through a large salad. Checking my watch, the amount of time left surprised me. I got a coffee, relaxing into the leisurely break. When I got back, they were already there. I was glad I hadn't mentioned their lateness in the morning; maybe they were feeling less ambivalent about our work now.

Emilia told the other two about her father.

Sebastian looked upset. 'Why didn't you tell us?'

Emilia shrugged. 'I suppose I didn't want you thinking I was unstable.'

'God, Emilia, we wouldn't think that. Why would we?' Sebastian said.

'You think I'm a dipstick, don't say you don't.'

'We think you're a bit scatty, and short-tempered at times, but not unstable. You're one of the most stable people I know,' Ben said.

'I wish you'd told us,' Seb repeated. 'Is that why you disappear sometimes?'

'I didn't know you noticed. Yes, sometimes I nip out to visit him,' Emilia said.

It was a sober ending to the day.

I took a detour through the park on my way to the tube. Wisps of cloud blew across the changing colours of the darkening evening sky. On the train home, I planned dinner, the phone calls I needed to make, until, from nowhere, a thought hurtled into my mind: I'd got the time for lunch wrong. I'd been fifteen minutes late. No wonder they were there already. How had I done that? Why didn't they say anything? Maybe

I hadn't been late after all? The more I thought about it the more confused I became. I rushed to my computer when I got home and started to write an email 'Was I late? Sorry if I was.' I deleted it.

Yes, they said, when I asked them at the beginning of our next session; you were late. I apologised. They hadn't said anything as they thought I might be paying them back for their lateness.

'That would have been mean of me,' I said. 'I certainly wasn't aware of doing that. I don't know what my unconscious was up to.'

Seb gestured with his hand, saying it didn't matter.

'It does matter,' I said. 'My lateness matters and trying to understand what may be going on unconsciously also matters. It helps to get at deeper issues.' They looked dubious.

Undeterred, I talked about not having mentioned their lateness at the beginning of the day. Instead of wondering with them what it meant and whether it expressed their ambivalence about the process, perhaps my lateness was an enactment of something left unspoken and unresolved.

'Like the stuff we didn't talk about for years, you mean?' Emilia asked.

I nodded. 'There does seem to be a big pile of stuff under the carpet.'

Seb stood up and sat back down, Emilia shuffled in her seat and Ben crossed his arms. Slowly, they identified the many unsaid issues over the years and the ways they may have been enacted. Seb forming an alliance with the founders from another agency and starting to negotiate a deal despite Ben and Emilia saying not to. In doing so, undermining their partnership and abandoning Ben and Emilia, instead of saying how hurt he felt by them abandoning him. Emilia's anger and occasional outbursts rather than telling them she felt marginalised and resented them treating her like an airhead. Ben stubbornly refusing to do anything in the evenings even when they had a deadline, instead of saying he wanted to reduce his hours. And the way it all affected morale and undermined all the agents' commitment to the agency and trust in the founders.

A couple of weeks later, I bumped into Seb with his wife and two children outside Tate Modern. He introduced me to his wife as 'the marriage counsellor at work'.

'I wish you wouldn't call her that,' his wife said.

'Me too,' I laughed.

He's right though, I thought, as we went our separate ways. The founders were like a married couple whose marriage had depended on burying their disagreements. Now, all the unspoken currents in the marriage overwhelmed them. Seb, feeling lonely and hurt, had fallen into the arms offered to him by the other agency. And everyone contemplated divorce.

At our next workshop, we explored the shift in their lives over the eight years since the agency's inception. 'Since we got married,' Seb said, telling the other two about how he'd introduced me to his wife. Just as the agency had evolved, so had they, as people.

'I wonder if you've allowed for the way you've each developed over the years. How your lives, priorities and dreams changed. And where you are in your lives now.'

'I suppose it really is like a marriage,' Seb said.

'We all seem to have done better in our actual marriages than in this one,' Emilia observed.

Feeling stronger now, they said they'd spend an evening together before our next workshop and discuss what they all wanted for themselves and for the agency going forward.

We had two more workshops. They were intense and turbulent; at times, as in most close relationships, harsh words were said that couldn't be taken back. I reminded myself that their passion indicated hate, rather than indifference. And hate has the potential to turn back towards love.

They made agreements: to stall the possible merger with the other agency, to meet monthly for lunch or dinner to rebuild their relationship as the founders and re-establish their threesome. They agreed that Emilia and Seb could take time to see and support their parents and Ben could reduce his hours. To achieve this, they would delegate more management responsibilities to other agents in the team.

We brought our work to an end with the understanding that they could ask for further sessions if they wanted. They were in a better place, though the marriage remained precarious. I hoped they had developed a more mature love for each other and the agency that would stand the test of time. I was unsure about the timing of our ending, but it was what they wanted and, at some point, marriage guidance counsellors have to get out of the way and leave the couple to get on with it.

Love can induce difficult feelings including jealousy and rage, but it also connects us with our best qualities, our most humane selves. It comes in many forms and shapes. Love for our work and love for the organisation as a whole which needs us, in the transient time we're there, to keep it alive. And the love in our affection, care and admiration for our colleagues.

Love can be inconstant, fluctuating, vacillating. It can be fickle, requiring attention, commitment and nourishment to keep going. Love can give way to hate, especially when unspoken issues poison the air and pierce its foundations. Love is found and lost. And love can be refound.

20

Speaking the Unspeakable

'Sixty-three murders so far.'

I stared out of the window, trying to take in my sister's email relaying the number of our relatives killed in the Holocaust. Sixty-three family members gassed, shot in the back of the head or wiped out through starvation or disease. Fifty more than we knew about, including many people that we hadn't known existed.

Wanting a project during the coronavirus lockdown of spring 2020, my sister was researching our family tree. Her choice of project made sense to me. The trauma of the virus evoked the trauma of our history: death suffused them both.

As the family tree grew and the number of our murdered relatives rose – reaching 136 by June 2021 – the silences surrounding our history became audible. I'd always been grateful to my parents, particularly my mother, for talking openly about their experiences, when I knew many others didn't. A cousin, for instance, only discovered he was Jewish and that most of his father's family had been killed in the camps when, at the age of thirteen, he asked to go on the school trip to Germany. His father's extreme reaction brought out the truth. Other relatives only found out they were Jewish in their twenties. A Czech Jewish friend and his non-Jewish

Danish wife hadn't told their children they were half-Jewish in case of another Holocaust. Since the line is passed from the mother, they thought the children's Jewishness might not be traced and so it would be safer for them not to know. The Jewish grandparents, both camp survivors, went along with the secret until their grandchildren were in their late teens.

I'd discovered that my father hadn't told my sister and me everything when I asked him to write his biography and for the first time learnt that two relatives had been gassed in Auschwitz. But even this omission hadn't prepared me for the gaps revealed by the family tree. I understood this but found it painful. The silence seemed to wipe out our relatives a second time.

During her research, my sister came across diaries that my father's cousin kept after the war. One entry described the impossibility of talking with a school friend who had survived a camp: 'her ghastly experiences, at which I can only guess, walked with us like a ghost, silent and sinister, at our side'.

Ghosts walked through all our lives. Some had names; most wove through us as invisible threads. A cloud of obfuscation surrounded them. Some 'facts' which had coloured our understanding of our family turned out to be myths. My uncle had not been the sole survivor of his large family. My aunt had not lost contact with my father and grandparents for ten years.

This blurring of history goes with the impossibility of processing such trauma and horror. The first generation could not begin to digest it, particularly since, like most people, they had no help. Silence was the only way of coping. Unsurprisingly, problems with mental health featured regularly in the family. My mother was finally diagnosed as bipolar at the age of seventy-eight. Perhaps she would always have had this illness, but the Holocaust undoubtedly increased her instability.

As extreme danger took over the external world and their own anxiety turned to terror, both sets of my grandparents, like other parents, became unable to contain their children's anxiety. Through no fault of their own, their inability to look after their children in this respect added to the trauma of my parents' generation.

We never thought of ourselves as Holocaust survivors. As a teenager, I challenged this, but my parents insisted the term only applied to those who had been in the camps. Their experiences, they said, did not compare. This strict hierarchy of suffering, established as an unquestioned norm by Jews in Palestine/Israel after the war, diminished my parents' experience. It also invalidated my distress.

The trauma hung around and in me, pulling on me in ways I was oblivious to. I inhaled it in the air I breathed, the feelings my parents projected into me unconsciously and the words that were not spoken. I only understood the extent and impact of it when I went into psychoanalysis.

Near the beginning of my analysis, my analyst referred to the 'concentration camp in my mind'. Stunned and outraged, I wanted to reject this, yet my unconscious instantly recognised that he had understood something beyond my grasp. Along with the shock and pain, I felt relief. The digestion process began. A process we returned to intermittently throughout my analysis.

One important moment occurred when I was giving a paper about Israel and Palestine to a psychotherapy organisation. I knew that many of the audience would be Jewish and feared their response, as criticism of the state of Israel often gets confused with antisemitism.

Two weeks before presenting the paper, I was enjoying an early morning espresso in my local café when I found myself on the verge of tears. I rushed home and was sick. I spent the day crying and trembling, a constant nausea in my stomach. At 6 p.m., I lay on my analyst's couch for my session.

'I seem to be more anxious about giving the paper than I'd thought.'

'I wouldn't call this anxiety. I'd call it terror,' he said.

I lay still as his words sunk in. 'It's Mum and Dad's terror isn't it? Terror about survival. This is transgenerational trauma,' I said.

'Um-hum.'

I had never experienced the trauma physically before. Weeping, I thought of the vastness of my parents' terror that couldn't be put into words and had passed to me viscerally. It coursed through my blood, my cells, affecting even my DNA.

My analyst and I came to understand that the 'concentration camp' part of my mind imprisoned me in nameless terror and pain. Wading through it, I began to articulate what we found there. The terror of death, an ever-present sense of guilt and shame and instant punishment if I tried to escape or infringe camp rules. Through it all, unmourned loss, passed down by my parents, relatives and our family ghosts, filled me with a seemingly unending grief.

In this part of my mind I had existed in a semi-dead state. A state not unlike the author David Grossman's description of 'the sense of doom that lies deep down in our [Israelis'] collective consciousness – that, for us, life is only latent death'.

I realised, to my shame, that without knowing it, I had carried the undigested weight of my history and our survivor status around like a trophy. Sometimes I took it out and showed it off to people. I didn't know what else to do with it. Since our background was rare in the UK, people often regarded my family history as exotic. Their awe reinforced and rewarded the trophy-like quality of my unprocessed trauma.

In putting my feelings into words, my analyst and I made

sense of the trauma and its affect. The trophy became integrated within, instead of sitting like a boulder on top of me. Mourning included disentangling my grief from the grief that had been handed to me, and the grieving I was doing on behalf of the family. Through digesting the trauma – as far as that is possible – we slowly liberated this part of me.

Writing this book, I realised that my history informed my becoming a consultant: helping people to speak the unspeakable, and so reduce the toxicity of secrets and silence, is an important part of what I try to do.

One team I worked with epitomised the shift from not speaking to speaking. They worked with high-risk borderline personality disorder patients in an NHS mental health trust. Most of their patients had experienced significant trauma and many had been abused. Self-harm and suicidality were common.

The team leader had recently left and one of the psychotherapists, Hamish, had temporarily taken over the role. There were two psychiatrists, Oliver and Naomi, and three other psychotherapists, Svetlana, Moira and Rob. Stress and sickness rates were high. Some posts remained vacant since financial cuts meant that, with the exception of the team leader, when staff left, they weren't replaced. As in other mental health services, cuts also meant that patients had to be more seriously ill than in the past. By the time they were seen, many were too ill to make use of therapy. Yet, the referrals kept coming and the waiting list increased day by-day. Despite working harder and harder, the team couldn't keep up with demand. They were anxious about the patients on the waiting list, as well as the ones they saw.

When I first met them for a diagnostic session, they talked about the impossible workload, the pressure of the waiting list and some gaps in communication between them, and between them and other teams both in and outside the trust. They worried that Hamish's position as team leader was only temporary. I found them open and engaged. It was only after the session that I realised they'd barely mentioned their patients.

In the programme I designed for a one-day workshop three weeks later, I included a slot about the impact of their work. When we came to this, I invited them to talk about the difficult feelings the patients evoked in them. They looked unsure but agreed to give this a go. As we sat in a close circle of chairs, they courageously put words to what had been hidden and unspoken. Svetlana opened the conversation. She told us about a man she was seeing.

'I feel such extremes. Warm towards him yet repelled. His history of abuse is horrific. Sometimes I don't know if I believe him. After our sessions, I block him out. It's the only way I can protect myself.'

'I find bearing witness to what patients have been through harrowing at times,' Naomi said. 'One middle-aged woman I've been seeing comes from a family with generation upon generation of horrendous abuse. It's hard to have any hope about her future. She can't. I try, but hope is so elusive.'

No one spoke. I looked at their faces filled with sadness.

Moira, the newest member of the team, continued. 'I feel completely without hope most of the time with one woman. Hopeless and useless. At the end of the fifty minutes, I'm so relieved to have got through another session. For months now, we haven't achieved anything. Yet, the risk is so high, I can't discharge her.'

'I get palpitations worrying about one suicidal patient,' Rob added. 'I wake up in the night fretting that I've missed something and it'll be too late.'

We paused. They filled themselves with coffee and cake as if making up for the depletion of their work. When we resumed, they talked about feelings of failure and guilt if patients deteriorated. Even when it was clearly not their fault, they felt that it was. Some felt guilty towards their families since when they got too stressed, they took it out on them. Others said they mostly managed not to take work home, but then worried that, like many of their patients, they'd cut off their feelings as a way of coping.

'We probably all do that at times but that's when we're most likely to miss things,' Hamish said.

Rob talked about feeling bored. 'One man bores me to death. I know it's an important communication from him, but I can't find the meaning and the boredom makes me want to give up. You're not meant to feel that are you?'

'I don't suppose you're alone,' I said.

Moira spoke about a suicidal woman. 'She's so damaged and her life is shit. I sometimes think she'd be better off dead. You're definitely not meant to feel that. No one ever talks about that.'

People nodded silently.

I had never heard a clinician say this before. Suicide is generally thought of as psychotic, so Moira's comment that it could be the right choice for the patient was brave. I smiled at her, touched by her candour and the team's receptiveness.

Rob said he'd become so used to self-harm that he'd look at cuts on a patient's arm and think, *is that all*? 'How awful is that?' he said. 'It's become so normal the level of self-harm has to be really severe before it makes any impression on me.'

'Our normal is dangerous,' Hamish said.

They described the pressure of knowing when to discharge a patient. Should they discharge people who weren't acutely suicidal? On the one hand, they needed to move patients on so they could decrease the waiting list. On the other hand, they were fearful about the risk.

Oliver stepped in. 'You don't have to decide risk alone. Your supervisor helps with that and you can always talk to me.'

'I don't think I'll cope if one of my patients kills themselves,' Svetlana responded.

'You will,' Oliver said. 'The risk is part of our work. Actually, it's amazing we haven't had more suicides.'

'You had one, didn't you?' she asked him.

'Yes, years ago. You never get over it. But it gets easier and you live with it.'

I admired his openness and honesty. But I was confused; given the team's preoccupation with it, I'd assumed one of their patients had killed themselves relatively recently. I was about to say this, when Naomi started speaking about a woman who, terrified of her suicidal thoughts over the Christmas break, had taken herself to hospital and tried to get admitted.

'It was such a healthy thing to do,' Naomi said. 'The part of her wanting to live took charge and tried to stop the part that wanted to kill herself. But the hospital wouldn't take her. I was furious when I heard, but of course they're as pressurised as the rest of us. They probably didn't have a bed.'

'And she's OK,' Hamish said, smiling at Naomi.

'Yes, she is,' Naomi agreed.

I sensed them detoxifying a little as the conversation continued. I still wondered why they were quite so preoccupied with suicide when they hadn't had one for so long. When I asked about this, Oliver commented that the team, in fact the whole trust, was far more gripped by the fear of suicide than any he'd worked for.

'I've never understood it,' he said. 'I know we take in our patients' suicidality – and this team probably has most of those patients – but even so. There haven't been more deaths in this trust than the average. And in the twenty years of this team's existence the only suicide was my patient ten years ago.'

'But there's been a lot of staff deaths in the trust,' Naomi said. 'Perhaps that's got something to do with it?'

A few years ago, three staff, all below the age of fifty, died within eighteen months. One had a fatal accident on his motorbike and two died of cancer. Those deaths in quick succession were particularly shocking, but plenty of other staff had died too. They speculated about the number of cancers among staff, assuming they were linked to the toxicity of the work.

Oliver reminded them of the trust's history and the awful time in 2006, before most of them were in post, when they merged with another trust and became a foundation trust as part of sweeping change in the NHS. A raft of staff left in a short time. 'The chief executive of the trust this team had been in went for the position of chief executive in the new foundation trust but didn't get it.' Oliver looked at me. 'He died not long afterwards. A heart attack. He was only fifty-five.'

'Staff must have been shaken,' I said, wondering if this was part of the backdrop to the fear.

Hamish shifted restlessly in his chair, worrying a scab on the back of his hand.

'I don't know whether I should say this or not,' he said. 'I only found out recently.'

'Found out what?' Oliver asked.

'You have to keep this to yourselves.' Hamish looked at them earnestly.

'What?' Oliver asked again.

'It may not have been a heart attack. It may have been suicide.'

'That can't be right. We've always been told it was a heart attack,' Naomi said.

Hamish explained that his family had wanted it that way but now his parents, who were the most concerned to cover up the suicide, were dead, it might be more possible to talk about it.

'Bloody hell. Is it true?' Moira asked.

'Looks that way,' Hamish replied.

He said that not getting the job might have been the last straw, but that it can't only have been down to that.

Naomi stared into the middle distance. Oliver shook his head.

'I'm stunned. But it explains the atmosphere and our constant anxiety,' Moira said.

I nodded. 'The trust had no choice but to keep it confidential if that's what the family wanted – and it's understandable – but it meant no one could process what had happened. Instead his death became part of the unconscious atmosphere staff soaked up.'

'Even those of us who joined years later and never knew the guy,' Rob said.

'We know that's what happens though. Trauma gets passed down through generations, particularly undigested trauma,' Oliver said.

We discussed the fear it had generated. Staff who had been around at the time must have worried that they had somehow caused or contributed to his death, perhaps through the additional stress and neediness they piled on him during the merger. Their anxiety about this will have activated the pre-existing unconscious guilt and wish for reparation that is part of many of us in the helping professions; a residue of the harm we fear we caused our loved ones in our inner world.

Before we ended, the team reflected on how much damage the secret had, in all likelihood, done in the trust and the relief of it being out in the open. They had also found talking together about the impact of their work helpful. They felt supported by their common experiences instead of alone with the acute pain and anxiety about their own case load. Each had thought they were the only one who sometimes had 'unacceptable' feelings about the patients. Knowing their colleagues had similar feelings lessened their guilt.

We set a date for a review session and said goodbye. I left, deeply moved by them, their work and their honesty and courage.

Three months later, we met for the review. The work was no easier and the patients as ill as ever, but Hamish had been made permanent team leader, so they felt more stable and secure. Since our workshop, they had begun to say no to some referrals and discharged more patients, which meant finally reducing the waiting list. They'd converted one team meeting a month to continuing the work we'd started, reflecting on the effect of their work and how each of them was feeling. Oliver summed up their progress:

'We've actually applied the "talking cure" to ourselves as a team.' He laughed. 'And in saying things we'd left unsaid and seemed unspeakable before, we're closer as a team and I think our resilience and mental health has improved.'

Driving home, my mind went back to transgenerational trauma. We tend to think of it as personal, as in my case; something that results from our ethnicity or family or from a personal tragedy. But trauma doesn't confine itself there. This team demonstrated that while transgenerational trauma in organisations isn't likely to be as far-reaching as personal trauma, it nonetheless has considerable power. I thought of the different organisations I'd worked in or with where trauma had a major effect. Sometimes the original cause was brutal cuts and fear of survival; other times it was badly handled mergers or takeovers. Or, as in this team, a specific, undigested incident.

Pushing trauma aside, whether stoically or defensively,

instead of speaking and digesting our experiences, affects existing staff in the workplace. It also affects future generations. Unknowingly, they are bequeathed an atmosphere suffocated by unidentified, unspoken emotions and nameless dread.

Over time and with help, I learnt to put words to my own nameless dread. Our past family trauma still affects me, and new traumas invariably resurrect the old one. But the Holocaust became part of my narrative with my own individual meaning. This helped me live with, rather than be controlled by trauma. And, as the silences and secrets took form and expression, hope was recovered.

21

Being Ourselves

I started coaching Diana two months after she became the director of a museum in York. When we spoke on the phone, she said her main goal for coaching was to create change in the museum. She was affable and open, telling me about her last job as senior curator in a museum in Liverpool. The position in York was a big step up and she wanted to ensure she made a success of it. She'd moved her home and family; her husband had got a partnership in a GP practice and the children were enrolled in new schools, but they hadn't wanted to leave Liverpool and were missing their friends.

'I owe it to them to get this right,' Diana told me.

Her boss, the chair of the board, had tasked her with increasing the museum's visitor numbers and getting new investment. Like the rest of the sector, the small amount of government funding they received had recently been reduced. Staying afloat was a major concern.

I agreed to meet her at the museum; it was an easy journey from London, and I looked forward to some time off in a lovely city. I tried to persuade her to see me off-site as I always do with coaching clients since a change of scene encourages different perspectives, but Diana, new to York, didn't know another suitable venue and was keen for me to come to the museum.

The first time we met, in late October, I arrived early. I sat on a bench near the museum entrance on a surprisingly warm day. Tourists went in and out of the ancient wooden doors, chatting to each other in many different languages. I went past a row of plane trees to the back of the museum and enjoyed going down the 'no unauthorised visitors' path to the staff entrance. Inside, the lobby was busy with the arrival of people and consignments. Diana's PA collected me and led me through a labyrinth of 'staff only' corridors and up three flights of stairs to a large office overlooking the city's rooftops.

Diana stood up from her desk and came forward to shake my hand, smiling warmly. She was petite with blonde hair framing her face. We sat down on the easy chairs to one side of the desk. She told me about her vision and the plans she was starting to form for new exhibitions that would increase visitor numbers while retaining the museum's mission. She spoke excitedly, flicking her hair out of her eyes as she spread the plans out on her desk to show me. I noticed a scar running across the palm of one hand.

She talked about the four senior curators who reported directly to her. They'd all been with the museum for many years. Two had applied for her job.

'They're being nice to me so far,' she said.

The previous director had retired after twenty-five years at the museum. He was well known and respected in the field, but conservative, and Diana didn't know what the curators would make of her plan to develop more outreach work with schools and build thematic interactive exhibitions, in collaboration with universities and private companies.

She was less worried about updating and expanding the museum's profile, than about bringing staff with her. She knew she had to start with the senior curators. We discussed what each one's concerns might be and how she could try to get them on board.

The one and a half hours passed quickly. We smiled at each other, both pleased at the end of our first session. I left brimming with excitement about her innovative ideas and looking forward to our next meeting.

When I returned the following month, I made sure I had plenty of time to look round the museum before our session started. It was quiet and tranquil, with a faint smell of varnish. I looked at the old paintings and some newer experimental works.

I felt nourished and relaxed as I entered Diana's office. She rose a fraction from her chair, as though standing up was too much trouble.

'Oh, do sit down,' she said, avoiding eye contact and indicating the easy chairs.

I tried to swallow some of the enthusiasm in my 'hello', which now seemed out of place. Perhaps, I thought, she's preoccupied or maybe something is wrong. She came around from behind her desk and sat opposite me. When I asked her what it would be helpful to focus on, she shrugged. I suggested we start with the curators, or her plans for change in the museum.

'OK.'

'Which one?' I asked. She looked weary and said it didn't matter.

The woman I'd met a few weeks ago had vanished. She'd become impenetrable. Finally, after several more questions, she told me she'd had a difficult meeting with one of the two curators who'd applied for her job. When Diana took up her post, he had been friendly and supportive towards her, but then became openly critical of her plans. He was the one we'd predicted would be the hardest to win over. I asked her what had happened.

In a flat tone, she told me that he'd pretty much laughed at some of her proposals, saying she didn't know the museum and certainly didn't know York. 'He said my plans are unworkable.'

'Do you think he's got a point or is it more about you getting the job instead of him?'

'I've checked with my old boss in Liverpool and he thinks my ideas are great and the guy doesn't know what he's talking about. But that's only one person.'

'How about the other curators?'

'I was going to ask them but, since getting that feedback ... Well, I haven't.'

She'd also put off talking to the curators about the balance between their work in and out of the museum. I had to press her to say more. Her eyes flitted away, as she explained that the curators carried out research and curated exhibitions for other organisations as well as the museum. This raised their profile and increased their knowledge and expertise. It also broadened the scope of their work, so was appealing. But these activities didn't bring in any revenue and, with the cuts and the urgent requirement to bring in more visitors, Diana thought the curators spent too much time on external activities.

Her look and tone conveyed that she found my questions tiresome and that she had answered out of politeness or obligation, rather than because she thought I could help her. It didn't seem the time to mention this, so I took up the theme of talking to the curators about balancing their work. I suggested she do this with them as a group, as well as individually, and gave her tips about how to engage them in the conversation. To my surprise, she smiled at me brightly, her voice suddenly upbeat, saying my suggestions were really helpful and she felt much more positive about having the conversations. But her words and tone seemed hollow and inauthentic.

I left the museum feeling depressed. The excitement from the first session had evaporated. I realised I'd worked considerably harder than Diana during the session, especially in my slightly overboard series of tips about talking to the curators. Perhaps, in part, my mood echoed hers as she moved beyond the initial excitement of starting the job, to the more depressed place where reality sank in. I was used to this; people often go through a honeymoon period and subsequent disillusionment in new jobs. But more than that, I felt an absence of any emotional contact between us. As if Diana was not present. I wondered if the engaging, charming woman I'd met before was a persona Diana hid behind. Today, that persona had deserted her, and the real Diana was hard to reach.

Travelling to York a month later, I felt slightly apprehensive. A thin sun added little warmth to the chilly day. I'd barely sat down with her, when Diana blurted out that she hadn't talked to the curators.

'I know, I know. I'm useless. You can see that now. I can't lead. They shouldn't have given me the job. I'm going to blow it. It's just a question of time before they realise. And then . . .' She stopped, brushed her hair out of her eyes and moved a pencil back and forth on the table.

'Sorry, I . . .' She stopped again.

The pencil made a scratching sound as she continued pushing it across the same small patch of table. I waited.

Finally, almost holding her breath, she spoke. 'I *cannot* fail in this job. It'll finish my career and I couldn't bear the humiliation.' She stared at her hands. 'It's a bit like school. A girl you thought was a good friend could suddenly turn on you.'

She looked wounded. I judged it more important at this moment to respond to the mention of school than her fear of failure. She said she'd had to move schools aged thirteen, when her parents split up.

'My brother stayed with Dad, and me and Mum moved to the other side of town. All the other kids had well-established friendship groups. I didn't know anyone. I was bullied. I begged Mum to let me go back to my old school, but she said it was too far away and I'd get used to the new one. In the end, I stopped asking.'

'Did you get used to it?'

She shook her head. I commented on how hard going to a new school, new house and not living with her father and brother must have been.

'It was. I missed my old life. Anyway ...' She stood up, walked over to the window. 'The thing about the curators is ...' she continued, her voice bright. Our conversation about school and family had ended.

In my mind, I saw a young Diana bullied and desperately unhappy in a new school. I pushed this aside for the moment, and asked what had stopped her talking to the curators.

She swept her fringe off her face impatiently. 'I thought they'd refuse point-blank to give up some of the external work and then I wouldn't know what to do.'

'So you prefer not to ask than risk your request being rejected?'

'Something like that.'

'Like asking your mum to let you go back to your old school?'

She stared at me. 'I hadn't made that connection.'

She returned to the table and rolled the pencil across it. 'The curators are much stronger than me. I—I won't be able to stand up to them.'

'What makes you think they're stronger than you?' I asked.

'I just know they are.'

I didn't say anything.

'I'll crumble.' She walked over to the window again, opening and closing it.

'I don't do well with criticism or attack. I crumble or run,' she continued, her back to me as she gazed out of the window. 'And I'm not good at reading people. What if I get that all wrong with the curators?'

'What about yourself? How are you at reading you?'

She turned round. 'Me? I can't do that either I suppose. I never know what I feel.'

It made sense; she'd seemed disconnected from her own feelings at our last session. If Diana's emotions often eluded and puzzled her, she'd find reading and understanding other people almost impossible. I wondered how it affected her marriage and parenting. I referred to school again, unsure how she'd respond. She told me she'd always hidden her feelings there since any sign of vulnerability provoked even worse bullying.

'But the crumbling is also a reaction to my father,' Diana said. 'He drank.' She looked at me as if gauging my reaction. I nodded.

'Then he'd have sudden outbursts of anger. He'd shout and throw things. Mum's constant refrain to me and my brother was *don't upset your father.* But when the drink took over … well, that was pretty impossible.'

She turned her palm to me. 'We were out on a walk. He'd been drinking and had lost it with me. I don't remember what I'd done. He yelled and yelled. I ran away and tripped and fell down a bank. I tried to break my fall with my hand and ended up cutting it on a rock and fracturing my wrist.' She examined her hand. 'I always tried, from a young age, to avoid him when he'd been drinking, but sometimes I couldn't.'

'Is that why your mum left with you?'

Dianna nodded. 'She tried to bring my brother too, but he refused. He was sixteen so I suppose Mum didn't feel she could make him. It was him I really missed when we left.'

After she and her mum moved, her dad's drinking got worse

and Diana saw less and less of him. Eventually, her brother moved out too, and went to live with his girlfriend's family.

'Dad still drinks now,' she murmured as the session came towards the end. She clamped her jaw shut and, in the remaining minutes, talked about the curators, telling me she'd try again to talk to them. This time, I thought she probably would.

Before getting the train back to London, I strolled by the River Ouse, went up the steps at a city gate and walked along a section of the ancient walls. Looking down into people's gardens, I thought about Diana as a child, frightened of her father, trying so hard to attune herself to him rather than the other way around. Maybe her mum couldn't really attune herself to Diana either because she too was preoccupied with trying to stop her dad from drinking. And then, as Diana entered the turmoil of adolescence, her world changed. Maybe she'd needed to cut off her feelings to cope.

The psychoanalyst Donald Winnicott talked about the 'true and false self'. We start to develop our 'true' self as a baby through our parents understanding our spontaneous gestures and expressions. We learn to trust our feelings and can explore ourselves and our world. The sounds and sights around us, how things feel against our skin, how they taste. We take in the reactions we get when we giggle, the look in our parents' eyes when they hold us. Perhaps Diana's parents, unable to do this, had misunderstood, ignored or curbed her natural expressions – not just sometimes as all parents do, but routinely. Diana would have doubted herself and instead of discovering who she was, adapted to what she thought her parents wanted.

At our last session, I'd felt she was complying, rather than engaging with me. Yet this time, she'd been emotionally present. I wondered which was more usual for her. If it was the absent compliance and, on the whole, she lived as a false self, coaching wouldn't help her. She'd need therapy. I was unsure, so decided to wait and keep an open mind.

At our next session, Diana told me she'd talked to the curators. It hadn't gone well. When the first one tried to discuss his external work for the museum, she'd assumed he was undermining her. She got angry and instructed him to reduce this work from now on. He'd stormed out of the meeting.

She pooh-poohed my suggestion that he may have genuinely not understood how outreach would increase numbers. I tried a different tack; how to get the best from the curators. Diana said that in Liverpool it was easy as there were only two other curators, and they automatically looked up to her because she was better qualified and had been there longer. It was different here and not knowing what to do, she'd adopted the behaviour she thought was expected from leaders: being in control and authoritative.

She's not alone in this; new leaders often try to copy role models. But usually when I ask them about it, they can articulate how it made them feel, whether powerful or fraudulent or like a toddler taking their first steps. Diana didn't have any idea how it made her feel. All she knew was that her firmness was followed by crumbling, as she put it, and she gave way. She changed her message and told the curators they didn't need to do more outreach work. In doing this, she'd unwittingly rewarded the curator for storming out of her office. Her vacillating behaviour must have left her team confused and, like me, doubtful about her ability to lead.

It seemed her 'false' self didn't know what to do with any questioning of her persona. She was trying to mimic being a leader and, even when the mimicry went well – and it often didn't – couldn't sustain it. I had to talk to her about therapy.

When I mentioned it, Diana thought I was telling her she was mad. I reassured her that I didn't think she was mad at all; I didn't see therapy as only for 'ill' people, but something many of us find helpful. She said she'd think about it. A few days later she emailed and asked me to recommend someone for her.

We agreed to put coaching on hold while she settled into therapy; she could take it up again if and when she wanted. Eight months later, she contacted me saying the therapy was helping and she'd like to resume coaching alongside it.

When we met again, nearly ten months after I'd last seen her, Diana leapt up to greet me, a broad smile on her face. The warm woman had returned. Therapy, she said, was helping her find out who she was, not who she thought she ought to be. It wasn't fast, but she could already see some changes.

'Last week the curators asked me a question I couldn't answer. I wouldn't have coped with that before. I'd have felt awful and either run or lashed out at them. This time, without crumbling, I said I didn't know but that I'd try to find out.'

'It sounds as if you can deal with not knowing everything and even being a bit vulnerable now,' I said.

'That's something isn't it?' She grinned.

'It is.'

'The best bit was the curators didn't attack me for it. I think they actually liked it.'

'You became more human,' I said, smiling at her.

I smiled to myself too as I saw that in starting to discover and develop her 'true' self, Diana was becoming emotionally present to herself and others. She could tolerate vulnerability and some uncertainty. The mimicry was on its way out. Now, we could start coaching.

22

Kindness

'Will it kill me?' Lottie asked, on getting the diagnosis of a slow-moving, but incurable blood cancer.

'We don't know,' the registrar replied. 'You're young to get this and unfortunately that gives it plenty of time to progress.'

'The hardest thing is living with the uncertainty,' the clinical nurse specialist added.

Lottie had returned to the hospital three weeks after first seeing the consultant haematologist and having tests. Sitting in the small shabby room, her ex-husband next to her, the registrar and nurse explained that the cancer wasn't caused by anything she'd done, and neither could she do anything to prevent its progress. Since they didn't know how long she'd had it, they couldn't predict its speed.

'It's like having one photograph from a whole series; as we take more photos, we'll see the pattern and have a clearer idea of what to expect,' the registrar told her. It could be years before she needed chemotherapy. When she did, it would reduce the cancer for a while. When it caused too much damage again, they'd give her more chemotherapy, but subsequent courses would be less effective than the first one, until eventually it would stop working.

Matthew, the clinical nurse specialist, gave her a leaflet and his card and told her to ring him with any questions or if she just wanted to talk.

As they came out of the room, Lottie saw the consultant nearby. He recognised her and gently asked how she was.

'Not great,' Lottie said.

'I wish I could just bring you in every three months to monitor you, without telling you why, but I can't.'

Speaking about this with me later that evening, Lottie commented on the consultant's kindness. 'He wanted to spare me from the psychological difficulty of this useless knowledge.'

Although we now lived in different parts of the UK and often went for months without talking to each other, Lottie and I remained close. We had been at university together and she was one of my oldest friends. We'd started speaking regularly when Lottie's GP referred her for a fast-track haematology appointment after an unrelated, routine test revealed something amiss.

It wasn't just the enormity and terror of the diagnosis, Lottie told me, during one of our many conversations in the weeks following her diagnosis, it was also other people's reactions. The kindness and unkindness, the thoughtfulness and thoughtlessness.

Her ex-husband kindly clearing his diary and accompanying her to get the results. A colleague – not even a close one – ringing her later. Friends rearranging meetings and childcare so they could be with her that afternoon and evening. A friend she met for coffee a week later bringing her a bunch of flowers. All of them letting her express her fear and not trying to diminish it or wave it away.

Other friends couldn't manage this and their unkindness, at this time of Lottie's acute vulnerability, hurt. Some kept their distance, as though she was contagious or contact with her brought them too close to their own mortality. One friend excluded her from a regular event. Another told her to forget the cancer and, when Lottie said that monitoring every three months made this tricky, told her not to go to the appointments. A relative sent her money to treat herself but quickly changed the subject if Lottie expressed any fear.

'Am I meant to be grateful for his bountiful gift? Buy a nice frock to make up for cancer?' Lottie asked me. 'The money has got nothing to do with generosity and everything to do with making him – not me – feel better.'

The thoughtless acts of unkindness added to the loneliness of the diagnosis.

Just before her sixtieth birthday, Lottie decided to treat herself to an 'anti-ageing facial'. The salon asked about any medical conditions and, to her dismay, refused to give her the facial when she told them about the cancer.

'I felt like a leper. They didn't even ask what sort of cancer I had. Suddenly I was untouchable.'

At her next 'watch and wait' monitoring, she told the consultant. He offered to write a letter to the salon so Lottie could have the facial. 'And if anyone asks you that again,' he advised, 'don't tell them about the cancer.' He turned to the three medical students, who had joined them for the appointment, 'Oh, I shouldn't say that, but it's ridiculous.' Turning back to Lottie, he clarified, 'People only need to know if you're going under the knife.'

'So can I have Botox?'

'My darling,' her consultant, twenty years her junior, replied, 'you don't need Botox, but if you want it, enjoy it.'

'Actually, what is Botox?' The medical students beamed at Lottie, trying to stifle their giggles. The consultant explained. And he explained about fillers and laser treatment too.

'If you want them,' he repeated, 'enjoy.'

'His kindness makes such a difference,' Lottie told me. 'I know Botox is vain, but he doesn't make me feel bad. He completely gets the psychological stuff behind the cancer.' He didn't judge her, or suggest she was wasting his time with trivia. She knew how busy he was; his secretary had mentioned that he was double-booked almost all the time. Yet, he never made her feel hurried and always took the time to ask her about her life, not just the cancer.

Lottie mentioned to one of the registrars how lucky she felt to be under this consultant. The registrar said she also felt lucky as he was great to work for. In modelling kindness, the consultant encouraged his team to display their own kindness. Once the hospital postponed one of the monitoring appointments by a month. Lottie rang her consultant's secretary to check the delay wasn't risky. Half an hour later Matthew, her nurse, rang, saying he'd heard she was concerned about her appointment. He talked it through with her.

'What fantastic care,' Lottie said to me. 'They're so thoughtful, so careful to try to reduce my anxiety.'

On another occasion, one result hadn't come back from the laboratory when she went for her appointment. She agreed with the registrar that she'd ring Matthew for it in a couple of days, but at 5.45 p.m. the registrar rang her. 'The results just came through,' she said. 'I thought you'd like to know.'

I was staying with Lottie for the weekend and we were talking about her experience over a bottle of Malbec. I suggested that the kindness, care and good relationships her medical team forged with their patients must be two-way. It would give staff pleasure and help them do their jobs. If Lottie was anything to go by, it also meant patients tolerated inevitable hiccups or delays.

Unkindness, I realised as Lottie and I talked, had been the currency in one of my jobs. When I started, I emailed my colleagues to see if they could suggest any potential contacts to help me generate work; not one of them replied. Targets bred competition and contacts became a commodity guarded jealously by each individual. The monthly staff meeting with its ritual naming and shaming of how we'd each performed against the targets, reinforced this. On my last day in the office, with no date for my leaving do, I thought some of us might go for lunch, but my colleagues, desperate to meet the targets, were out seeing clients. I cleared my desk and went alone for a sandwich. Coming back after lunch I saw a beautiful bunch of flowers on the reception desk. I immediately cheered up, appreciative of this thoughtful gift.

'Do you like the flowers we got for Emily?' my boss asked as she saw me looking at them. The repair undid and I recoiled inwardly. Emily was in favour at the time, but it didn't last. The mean, thoughtless, unkindness in the department left each of us alone, isolated in the shell of a team.

Adam Phillips and Barbara Taylor in *On Kindness* trace the evolution of kindness through history and the impact of political systems. 'Capitalism,' they say, 'is no system for the kind-hearted.' As Thatcherism radically changed UK society during the 1980s, kindness became a weakness and care-giving a demeaned, badly paid occupation. Competition without restraint permeated society. 'A competitive society, one that divides people into winners and losers, breeds unkindness.'

In the early days after her diagnosis Lottie imagined that every small pain or symptom was the cancer. Yes, her consultant told her, when she mentioned nose bleeds and sinusitis. 'You'll get more of those now.'

'What about the itching in my ears?' she asked.

'Irrelevant,' he replied. His directness made Lottie laugh. She could discard this particular symptom but more than that, his honesty and straightforwardness built trust.

Coronavirus brought unexpected challenges for Lottie. The cancer was true to its 'indolent' nature and she remained well. Finding herself in the 'clinically extremely vulnerable group', shocked her and all of us close to her. She'd known she might become very ill one day and need chemotherapy, but now the reality of her reduced ability to produce antibodies struck home.

As a member of this group, she got frequent texts from the government. The first one panicked her. 'You can open a window,' it said. 'But you must not leave your property. Get other people to take the rubbish out . . .'

A few days later a text advised her to pack a small bag in case she needed to go to hospital. Lottie rang Matthew to check what this all meant in her case. Getting no answer, she didn't leave a message. A while later a man rang her saying she'd tried his number. He turned out to be Danny from Heathrow airport, absolutely nothing to do with Matthew, at the hospital. If Danny hadn't taken the trouble to ring her back, she wouldn't have known she'd got Matthew's number wrong.

Danny's small act of kindness was one of so many during the pandemic, especially at the beginning. Despite the instruction to stay at home, Lottie couldn't get online deliveries for the first few weeks. She rang the local small supermarket that had started deliveries in the area. When she explained her situation, the man she spoke to told her to email her shopping list as that would be quicker than using the website. He rang back later to get payment and her address. Realising he lived near her, he told her to ring and ask for him if she needed anything as he could drop it off on his way home from work.

The sense of togetherness created by a common, mortal enemy assists kindness. Coronavirus also brought us face to face with our mortality and dependence on one another. While some depended on others for their daily needs, we all depended on one another to stop the spread of the virus. Comforting illusions of omnipotence and independence fell apart. And as it did, kindness could develop. Because kindness can only exist if we acknowledge our frailty and interdependence. As Phillips and Taylor say, 'Acts of kindness demonstrate, in the clearest possible way, that we are vulnerable and dependent animals who have no better resource than each other.'

Kindness, whether to those we love, our colleagues or complete strangers, rewards us by reminding us of our better selves. It gives expression to our generosity and our empathy. We feel helpful and useful. We step beyond ourselves and put others first.

Imagine if we deliberately sought to create kindness at work. If we used it as a descriptor, a measure of well-functioning teams and workplaces. Not a false camouflage of polite niceness, but real kindness in which workplaces accept and deal with our meanness, cruelty, hatred and envy, and allow for our vulnerability, need and dependence. And in accepting all that we are, favour our capacity for kindness; our wish to look out for and connect with others.

During the pandemic, Lottie turned to another kind figure in her life, her psychoanalyst. She'd finished analysis, but they had a session on Zoom. Lottie expressed her mortal fear and the loneliness of prolonged self-isolation. In his presence she understood that what made this so difficult, so fraying, was what happened in her inner world. She'd returned to the helplessness of being left alone to the terrors of infancy by her unthinking, emotionally neglectful parents. Alone in the dark, hungry, hearing indecipherable noises; alone with her rage when no one came. Her insight reminded her that she wasn't an infant but had the resources of her adult self. And she wasn't alone but had the kindness and support of her analyst, her medical team, her friends and family.

23

Looking Back to Move Forwards

Claudette, the headteacher, waited for me at the end of the corridor. The familiar scent of her perfume, Rive Gauche, wafted past as we went into her light and tidy office.

She sat down wearily. Her red necklace, striking against her deep brown skin and elegant grey fitted dress, contrasted with the dark circles around her eyes. Pouring coffee, she said George, the deputy headteacher, would join us shortly. 'I've told the staff about the change programme every step of the way, so why do they insist on having amnesia and go back to the old ways of working?'

I'd run some workshops on leadership with the senior team two years earlier. I hadn't heard Claudette's sour tone before.

Books, interspersed with cacti and spider plants, lined two walls of the office. A tall glass-fronted cabinet housed box files and folders, opposite a large, uncluttered, desk. The vase on the meeting table, usually full of fresh flowers, stood empty.

Serving a predominantly working-class community, pupil numbers were rising. Because of this and their consistent Ofsted grade as an outstanding school, they'd expanded the number of classes and created year leaders to replace subject leaders and so provide a more robust middle management tier. Seven year leaders would sit between the senior leadership team – the head, deputy and three assistant headteachers – and the rest of the staff. The first three year leaders had started four months ago. The other four would join them over the next two terms.

Claudette had rung me wanting help with the change process. She'd insisted the only problem was that the year leaders hadn't taken on their responsibilities and continued to operate like team members, not leaders. For instance, when an eight-year-old boy refused to do his work, instead of going to the year leader, both the form teacher and the assistant head teacher went straight to George.

'Oh,' she'd said, while I was trying to understand why that was the year leader's fault, 'I have to rush now but just to let you know, George's retiring next year.'

My mind had raced. George and Claudette had worked together for decades. They met each morning for coffee and went through the day ahead. They often ate lunch together and checked in on each other before going home. Their division of labour kept everything running like clockwork; she led the senior leadership team and handled the governing body, local authority and key external groups, while he focused on managing and mentoring the teachers and difficult parent issues. She could be stern when needed; he complemented her as the softer support figure. He'd supported her during the slow battle to gain acceptance as a black headteacher.

'I trust him completely. He knows what I'm thinking without me telling him and he's always got my back,' she once told me. Everyone – staff, pupils, parents – joked about the two of them being like a married couple.

Now, George came in through the interlinking door between their offices. He greeted me affectionately, helped himself to coffee and sat down at the table. Older than Claudette, his habitual tweed jacket and creased face always reminded me of the kindly, benevolent grandfather in children's stories.

They'd made a meticulous plan for the change process. As they talked me through it, I found myself getting lost in the detail. I realised I had no idea how they felt about it. 'It's simple,' Claudette said. 'We're expanding. The changes have to happen.'

'That doesn't make it easy,' I said, 'especially perhaps for the teaching staff.'

'We wouldn't be introducing this if we didn't think it was right.' George sounded irritated. The two of them exchanged looks.

They launched into the gains of having year leaders. 'It's really positive. We're embracing change,' George said, sitting back expansively.

My heart sank. I heard this Pollyanna mantra so often. Why, if everything was so good, had Claudette said the change wasn't working? I asked about the incident with the child who wouldn't do his work. 'Surely it wasn't the year leader's fault that the form teacher went to the assistant head and not to her?'

'She should have made it clear to her team to come to her. She's too passive,' Claudette replied sharply.

I wondered about this new impatience. 'You seem annoyed.'

'Of course I am,' she retorted.

I felt stuck, unable to understand or ask what was going on with her.

I asked George what he'd done when the form teacher and assistant head came to him. He'd spoken to the boy. The irony of his exclusion of the year leader seemed to escape them. They acknowledged that they'd only involved her afterwards.

'It's hard isn't it,' I said. 'Hard for everyone, including you two, to include the year leaders and resist the default position of everyone coming to you – or you sorting everything out between yourselves.'

The phone rang. Claudette picked it up. 'I said no interruptions,' she snapped.

George glanced at me.

I suggested that giving up their regular contact with the teaching staff might be difficult. George said he already missed hearing about their everyday lives; a squabble at home, what they did at the weekend, how their children were getting on, problems with ageing parents. It made him feel close to them.

'You're losing that,' I said. 'Loss is always part of change.'

'Really?' Claudette asked.

'None of the change management books I read mentioned that,' George said.

I kept trying to bring up the impact of his retirement but they batted it away.

'That's ages away,' Claudette said dismissively.

George glanced quickly at me again. 'I haven't even set a date,' he said.

'But it's next year isn't it?' I asked. He nodded. 'That isn't *that* far away,' I said.

Claudette brushed this aside. They insisted there was plenty of time to work it all out.

I met with the assistant headteachers and the year leaders to talk about the change with them. The assistant headteachers seemed confused and felt peripheral to the change process. The year leaders, having been promoted internally, were anxious and isolated in their new roles. I wondered what had happened to Claudette's usual ability to involve and support her team.

Claudette came to see me at my consulting room a week later. Normally punctual, she arrived thirty minutes early. She stood on the doorstep dripping with rain. Red rims around her eyes added to the dark circles. Her normally rich skin tone looked dull.

I made coffee. 'How are you?' I asked, putting the mug on the side table beside her.

'Fine.'

'Are you?'

'Yes.' I looked at her. 'I've got a few personal things going on, but I'm OK,' she said.

We discussed plans for the change process, the need to support the year leaders and help them adjust to their new role. I brought up George's retirement, thinking she might find it easier to talk about without him there, but she wouldn't be drawn. Previously, I'd have commented on her reluctance, but now I didn't feel I could.

A week later Fayola, one of the assistant head teachers, rang me. Did I know, she asked, that Ofsted would be inspecting them very soon? They'd just been told. On top of this, two exceptional teachers had resigned. They'd told Fayola they hadn't planned to go but their new jobs offered a great opportunity. And they were losing confidence about the future direction of the school as Claudette wasn't herself. 'I didn't know what to say. They're right. Something's wrong with Claudette.'

When George came for his individual session, he immediately told me about the pending inspection.

'It's always stressful,' he said, 'but now . . .'

'Now?' I asked.

He shook his head. 'What will happen if . . .' He stopped, turning his face away.

I felt, as I had with Claudette, that I needed to tread

carefully. I asked how he felt about retiring. Although he'd made the decision, he couldn't imagine life without the job he loved. He feared endless days with nothing to do.

'Who will I be when I'm no longer deputy head teacher?' He shook his head as if shaking off bad thoughts. 'But that's not the point,' he continued quickly. 'It's the year leaders. Maybe we made the wrong appointments. And what if Claudette doesn't find a good replacement for me? Perhaps this is just the wrong time for me to retire. But then that's not fair on my wife. We've spent years planning for this.' He paused, squeezing his hands together.

I said that the year leaders had only just started. Perhaps they just needed the chance to develop. George calmed down a little.

'What about your replacement? I know there's a shortage of leaders coming through the system. Are you worried you won't get good applicants?'

'No, not really. The school's got such a good reputation, lots of people would jump at the chance to work here,' he said. 'Unless we suddenly get a bad Ofsted – and you never know – but I'm not really worried about that.'

'So this is more about your anxiety and perhaps guilt about leaving Claudette?'

George adjusted his glasses, took them off and cleaned them. Putting them back on, he spoke so quietly I could barely hear him.

'When I was seven, my father died. Mum didn't cope. That's what I didn't say before; what if I have to pick up the pieces like I had to with my mother when my father died. I can't retire yet.' We sat together, still and silent.

The following month, I ran a workshop with Claudette and George, the assistant heads and the year leaders. With no other room available, we sat on small children's chairs around small tables. Brightly coloured pictures, each carefully signed in a childish hand, decorated the walls. Animals, flowers and trees, sun and snow joined mums and dads, siblings and grandparents and an array of multi-coloured vehicles.

They described the change process with metaphors. Claudette and George visualised a large ship, with them at the helm. There was a good navigation system and enough food and fuel for the journey. They regularly informed the crew of the longitude and latitude, any deviations from the route and expected time to port. The assistant heads hovered close by, but the rest of the large crew mostly stayed below deck and ignored the information Claudette and George gave them over the tannoy. Occasionally they threw heavy objects into the sea that obstructed the ship's progress.

The year leaders described a road without end that either led to green pastures or went straight over a cliff. They and their teams walked along or rode in buses. The teams kept asking questions the year leaders couldn't answer. Now and again, they saw Claudette and George and the assistant heads up ahead and, periodically, one of this group came back and talked to them and their teams. Sometimes though, when the year leaders needed help, they couldn't find anyone to ask.

The assistant heads associated the change process with a river. In good weather they enjoyed the clear, clean water and could see the different-shaped and sized rocks on the riverbed. People scattered the surrounding countryside. After a heavy rainfall the river overflowed and filled with mud from the banks. The muddy water became treacherous as it sped past, veiling the riverbed and hiding deadly fish.

It struck me that none of the metaphors had a leadership team. They were taken aback and slightly embarrassed when I pointed this out. We talked about the undifferentiated people in the assistant heads' metaphor, who could be leaders, staff, pupils or parents. Or maybe they had nothing to do with the school. In the year leaders' metaphor, the senior leaders came and went, giving them inconsistent and unreliable support. The year leaders themselves remained with their teams, disconnected from the other leaders. And in Claudette and George's description, the two of them ran the ship alone. The assistant heads hovered nearby without a role. The year leaders morphed into the mass of the crew hidden, for the most part, under deck and attempting to subvert the ship's progress.

Their metaphors told of a lonely and perilous change process. The assistant heads clung together, as did Claudette and George and the year leaders. Each subgroup felt isolated and disconnected from everyone else. We could see the poor teamwork, but also the difficulties with distributed leadership. It was unclear how the year leaders fitted with the assistant head teacher roles and what authority each had. The lack of clarity left everyone confused and made accountability impossible. Yet, no one had asked for elucidation.

'You haven't mentioned loss,' I said. 'I suspect that not talking about it has made it harder for you to pull together as a team.'

Claudette's eyes welled up. She looked away when she saw me looking at her. We talked about the loss of clarity and how by passively accepting, rather than questioning the blurred roles, they'd unwittingly sabotaged change.

We stopped for coffee. Nick, one of the assistant headteachers, handed round cake left over from his birthday the day before. The team teased him; just as well he was giving them the cake given his expanding waistline. Another year, another inch or four.

After the break, the year leaders tentatively acknowledged feeling exposed in the new roles and missing the familiarity of their old jobs and their friendships with peers. The assistant heads missed their former certainty too; they no longer knew exactly where they were in the hierarchy. They missed some of the day-to-day interaction with the teaching staff. Claudette and George talked about the hole left by the loss of contact with the staff. They also recognised how much they feared losing control through distributing leadership.

'Despite our careful preparation and planning, or maybe even because of it, we missed the fact that feelings don't always follow plans,' Claudette said.

'I don't think we really allowed for feelings at all,' George added.

No one, I said, had mentioned George's retirement.

'It's the biggest loss,' Fayola said. They didn't talk about it because they found it unsettling and, Nick added, they weren't sure it would really happen. Fayola turned to Claudette. 'Mainly though' – she swallowed – 'we don't say anything, or I don't anyway, because I'm worried about upsetting you.'

'I had no idea you felt like that.' Claudette looked dismayed. 'I do find George leaving hard, but I'm OK. You don't have to treat me with kid gloves. I really don't want that.'

Everyone looked at George. He paused before speaking, his Adam's apple contracting. 'It's a huge step for me but I'm definitely retiring. I prevaricated about the date because I was a bit unsure. I didn't think about the effect on you though.' He promised to confirm the date by the end of the month.

The following week, Claudette came to see me for another session. She took a few sips of coffee before setting the mug down. She tucked her hair behind her ears and pulled at her skirt, exhaling slowly.

'My husband has left me. He's been having an affair for two years. He wants a divorce.'

They'd been married for thirty years and brought up three children. They'd bought a new house five years ago and refurbished it, adding an extension and converting the loft. He'd project-managed the whole thing, acquiring a new-found interest in design.

'I feel so deceived, so betrayed,' Claudette said. 'I didn't know. How could I not know?' She pulled at her skirt again. 'I believed our marriage was forever. He doesn't even seem to care about what this will do to the children. How can he be so selfish? A younger woman. Some nubile bitch. Beauty. I mean beauty.'

'Calling her a bitch seems fair enough,' I said.

'I don't want to become bitter,' Claudette said. 'I used to manage someone like that. Always complaining. So bitter and twisted. It's not a good look.' We both laughed.

'I bet my husband's "*lover*" doesn't have stretch marks or dyed hair.' She paused, all at once looking utterly forlorn and lost. 'I'm not young; I don't know how to start again. I'm terrified of being on my own.'

'I'm so sorry,' I said.

Claudette's husband hadn't died but her marriage had. Her workplace marriage was also ending. No wonder, when facing so much loss herself, she'd been unable to help the staff and school address loss. She was seeing a counsellor and I hoped that with support, she'd be more able to do this now.

In *Mourning and Melancholia*, written during the First World War, Freud noted that melancholia – severe depression in today's language – shares the same characteristics as mourning. In both, we become lethargic and disinterested in the world around us. Mourning the death of someone close to us is extraordinarily hard work. Consciously and unconsciously we trawl our memories of them so we can detach from them and face, bit by bit, again and again and again, the fact that they're no longer here. Without mourning we can become prone to long-term depression.

No one had died in the school, but if they didn't address their loss, they risked organisational depression which would block change. By allowing and talking about their feelings, the leadership team were mourning. They now needed to create spaces for the rest of the staff to do the same. Not endlessly – this was a workplace not a therapy centre – but enough.

The next time Claudette came to see me she looked brighter. She'd told the wider leadership team about her divorce. She desperately missed her old life. 'I'll be a divorced woman. I never imagined that.' She'd miss George too. And she knew he'd miss his career. 'We're probably all a bit destabilised by the changes. I certainly am.'

'You wouldn't be human if you weren't,' I said. 'Loss and grief are destabilising.'

I thought about the struggle Claudette faced to mourn her old life and the end of her marriage, while leading the school through change. And how hard it would be for her and the whole school to detach from George enough to give his replacement a chance.

Claudette continued coming to see me intermittently over the next two years. She and the children spent the summer in Jamaica, where she let her relatives lavish them all with care. The divorce came through and she picked up the pieces and started to build a new life for herself. She worked hard to emotionally let go of George in time to help him retire well. It was probably inevitable that she didn't take to the young woman who replaced him, but in time Claudette came to respect her and they formed a different, but solid pair, as they led ongoing change in the school. She mourned in her private life, and she and the school found their way to mourn too.

The gruelling work of mourning requires us to stay connected with the past, live in the present and look forward to the future; to honour history and memories, without turning events and places into monuments and people into ghosts.

At the End

Endings are rarely given the importance they deserve. They matter. Good endings help us move to new beginnings; they open up a space for something as yet unknown. Bad endings keep us stuck; they can lead to repetitive cycles in which space diminishes.

Endings mark the passage of time: as we go towards the future the present recedes to the past. Yet, as William Faulkner says, and the stories in this book show, 'The past is never dead. It's not even past.' It is this conflation of tenses in our minds, our lives and in our workplaces that lend endings their weight.

The rituals of endings – funerals, wakes, leaving parties – help us honour, mourn and celebrate what was. Endings at work are about our relationships with colleagues and clients, about the work we do and that part of our life and identity. To differing degrees, all endings involve mourning.

In my work endings vary enormously; I'm not sure my clients always realise that the ending is a process with an impact and a loss (and, on rare occasions, some relief), for me, as well as for them.

But how do you end a book? How do you decide when it is, to use Winnicott's phrase, 'good enough'? And how do I say goodbye to you, the reader, who I haven't met but have had in my mind for many years during the writing of this and its evolution to this final form? I don't know.

I do know though, that this book's themes can be found in workplaces far beyond those described here. Because although each case study in this book is unique, in stripping away the layers and getting to the heart of all that we are, they are also universal. And I know that behind the characters are a great many more of my clients. In the commonality of their humanness, I like to think that you have seen parts of yourself too.

Writing this book led me to many discoveries; some of them about pieces of work long since completed that I understood better. Some of them about myself. Along the way, I also discovered the joy of writing.

I hope in reading this book you, too, have made discoveries – about your organisation, or yourself, or the enigma of human nature and the way our internal and external worlds always interrelate. I hope you leave this book with no illusions about human nature and the cost of ignoring it in the workplace, yet also uplifted by the potential of all that we are.

Notes

Introduction: Starting With Us

Thriving at Work: The Stephenson/Farmer Review of Mental Health and Employers (2017), Department for Work and Pensions and Department for Health and Social Care, UK Government.

'Health and safety at work. Summary statistics for Great Britain 2019', Health and Safety Executive (HSE).

France Télécom: the trial against France Télécom found that between 2008 and 2010 nineteen employees committed suicide, twelve attempted suicide and another eight employees were unable to work due to depression or other reasons related to the company's restructuring after privatisation. It was the first time a French court found a company guilty of 'institutional harassment'. The chief executive and two other executives were found guilty of 'moral harassment' and four other executives found guilty of 'complicity'. (BBC News, 20 December 2019 and France24 with AFP, Reuters, 20 December 2019.)

UK Post Office: between 2000 and 2014, the Post Office prosecuted 736 sub-postmasters and sub-postmistresses (branch managers) for theft, fraud and false accounting after its new computer system erroneously recorded discrepancies. Rather than investigating the system, the Post Office blamed individual sub-postmasters and postmistresses. Six former sub-postmasters and sub-postmistresses had their convictions overturned in December 2020 and another 39 had their convictions quashed by the Court of Appeal on 23 April 2021. Some had served prison sentences, many went bankrupt, losing their livelihoods as well as their homes. Some have since died. (Haroon Siddique and Ben Quinn, 'Court clears 39 post office operators convicted due to "corrupt data"', *Guardian*, 23 April 2021.) More cases will be referred to the Court of Appeal and the Post Office is unlikely to contest them.

The Trades Union Congress (TUC) reported that in 2018 45 per cent of safety representatives ranked bullying and harassment second only to stress in their concerns about the workplace. It was highest in local and central government: in a survey, 80 per cent and 71 per cent respectively of respondents identified it as a concern. The TUC also found that bullying is most frequently directed against black and Asian employees, women and people with a disability. *Bullying at Work: Guidance for Workplace Representatives*, TUC, February 2019.

1: The Choices We Don't Know We Make

Lawrence, G. (1977), Management Development ... Some Ideals, Images and Realities. In A.D. Coleman and H.D. Geller (eds) (1985), *Group Relations Reader 2*, 1985, A.K Rice Institute Series.

Organisational purpose: building on Rice's concept of the 'primary task' – the task an organisation 'must do to survive', Rice, A.K. (1963), *The Enterprise and its Environment* (London: Tavistock Publications). Lawrence differentiated between three primary tasks:

'normative' (the official task the organisation needs to do)
'existential' (the task staff believe they're carrying out)
'phenomenal' (the task staff actually do but may be unaware of)

2: Safety and Security

Bowlby, J. (1967), *Attachment and Loss Volume 1: Attachment*. Pimlico. First published 1969 Hogarth Press and the Institute of Psychoanalysis.

Bowlby, J. (1988), *A Secure Base*, Routledge. First published in Routledge Classics, 2005.

Braun, G. (2011), 'Organisations Today: what happens to attachment?', *Psychodynamic Practice. Individuals, Groups and Organisations*, Volume 17, No. 2, 2011.

Braun, G. and Armstrong, D. (2015), 'Leadership of Thinking: What's Attachment Got to Do With It?' in *How can Psychoanalysis and Systems Theory Contribute to the Leadership of Thinking in the Further Education and Skills Sector?* Further Education Trust for Leadership, 2016.

Attachment theory: Bowlby thought that attachment has an innate biological and evolutionary function: just as young animals need their parents to guard them from predators, children need to stay close to an adult to be protected from dangers in the environment. Attachment is also psychological. 'The young child's hunger for his mother's love and presence is as great as his hunger for food.' (Bowlby, 1967, p.xiii.)

In 1969, Bowlby's colleague, Mary Ainsworth, developed the 'Strange Situation' to test attachment in twelve-to-eighteen-month-old children. The test is still used today. Ainsworth and her colleagues identified three attachment patterns:

Secure attachment: a strong psychological bond with their parents or carers, gives the child a 'secure base'. With this psychological security the child acquires appropriate independence and autonomy and can move away from their parents enough to explore and play.

Insecure avoidant: the child has been turned away or rejected regularly when they looked for care from their attachment figure, so has learnt that it is better not to attach to anyone. These children minimise their attachment needs and keep to themselves.

Insecure ambivalent: parents or caregivers have been unreliable – sometimes available and responsive, and sometimes not. There will often have been separations and the use of threats of abandonment to control the child. These children are always anxious about separation and, in contrast to insecure avoidant children, tend to cling to their attachment figure.

In 1986, Mary Main identified a fourth attachment pattern: *disorganised attachment*. Less common, this contrasts with the other two insecure patterns which are organised and based on interaction. In disorganised attachment there is no clear pattern or organisation of parent/child interaction. *Disorganised attachment* can lead to serious mental health problems.

3: Life and Death

Freud, S. (1920), Beyond the Pleasure Principle. In *The Standard Edition of the Complete Psychological Works of Sigmund Freud Volume XVIII* (1920–1922), Vintage, Hogarth Press and the Institute of Psychoanalysis.

4: Another Side of Aggression

Klein, M. (1932), The Psycho-Analysis of Children. In *The Writings of Melanie Klein, Volume* 2. First published, Hogarth Press, 1932, revised edition 1975. Published by Vintage 1997.

Obholzer, A. (1994), Authority, power and leadership. Contributions from group relations training. In *The Unconscious at Work: Individual and Organizational Stress in the Human Services*, Routledge.

Authority: Obholzer identified three sources of authority:

Authority from 'above': which is conferred on us by our job roles. It also comes from the authority given consciously or unconsciously, by those above us in the hierarchy;

Authority from 'below': for leaders, this is the authority given by those in their staff;

Authority from within: if we cannot find authority within ourselves, we won't be able to use the authority conferred by others.

5: The Looking Glass

Klein, M. (1946), Notes on some schizoid mechanisms. In *Envy and Gratitude, Volume 3. The Writings of Melanie Klein* (1975), London: Hogarth Press.

Carroll, L. (1872), *Alice's Adventures in Wonderland*, p 41 and *Through the Looking Glass, and what Alice found there*, Penguin Classics, 1998.

6: Barriers and Barricades

Bion, W. R. (1962) 'A theory of thinking', *International Journal of Psychoanalysis*, 43:306–10; republished (1967) in W. R. Bion, *Second Thoughts*, Heinemann.

Bion, W. R. (1962), *Learning from Experience*, Heinemann.

Brewer, Garry D. (1989), Perfect Places: NASA as an Idealized Institution. In Radford Byerly, Jr (ed.), *Space Policy Reconsidered* (Boulder, CO: Westview Press, 1989), pp.158 and 159–165, quoted in Columbia Accident Investigation Board report, p.102.

Menzies, I. (1959), 'The functioning of social systems as a defence against anxiety: a report on the study of a nursing service of a general hospital', *Human Relations*, 13: 95–121. Reprinted in Menzies Lyth, I. (1988), *Containing Anxiety in Institutions*, London: Free Association Books.

NASA (1986), *Report of the Presidential Commission on the Space Shuttle Challenger Accident*, pp.17 and 83. (Known as the Rogers Commission Report.)

NASA (2003), *Report of Columbia Accident Investigation Board, Volume 1.*

Waddell, M. (1998), *Inside Lives: Psychoanalysis and the Growth of the Personality.* First published by Gerald Duckworth & Co. Ltd, 1998. Third Impression, Tavistock Clinic Series, 1999.

Containment: in psychoanalysis, emotional containment is considered key to mental stability. It begins with the parent's capacity to receive anxiety projected into them by their baby. The parent tries to make sense of this communication so they can respond appropriately (for example, with soothing words and a cuddle after a nightmare or taking the baby away from a loud noise or changing their nappy). In doing this, parents communicate to the baby that their incoherent states of mind can be converted into emotions and thought about. The baby feels comforted and safe, and also, importantly, understood. In this way, the baby begins to establish an understanding, containing person in their own mind and so begins to also reflect on their own states of mind and feelings. As the psychoanalyst Margot Waddell says, 'Initially the mother [parent] thinks *for* the infant. Slowly the infant learns to perform that function for himself so that the mother, or parent, may think *with* him.'

Bion called the receptive state of mind the parent needs for containing their child 'maternal reverie'. If parents cannot reflect on their baby's state of mind (if, for instance, they are preoccupied with financial worries), or if the infant cannot use it (perhaps because of illness), the baby's anxiety spirals. Bion described the baby's terror when their parent cannot contain them as 'nameless dread'. Not only is the baby's original anxiety unmodified, but this is added to by the fear of never being understood or contained which will leave the baby in terrifying chaos.

In the workplace containing anxiety is a vital part of creating a healthy environment in which staff can function and work well.

7: Good Enough

Mike Brearley, 2016, in conversation.

Freud, S. (1933), New Introductory Lectures on Psychoanalysis. In *The Pelican Freud Library, Volume* 2 1973. Reprinted by Penguin Books, 1975 and 1977.

Winnicott, D. W. (1964), *The Child, the Family, and the Outside World*, Pelican Books, republished in Penguin Modern Classics, 2021.

The superego: this is part of Freud's model of the mind from his later work. The model has three components: the 'id', 'ego' and 'superego'. The id is largely unconscious. It is the home of our instincts and some of our irrational, extreme and contradictory desires and emotions. The term 'ego' in psychoanalysis refers to the largely conscious part of our mind that tries to bridge and mediate between the superego and the id. One of its key functions is to adapt to reality – something neither the id nor the superego concern themselves with. 'The poor ego', Freud said, 'serves three harsh masters and does what it can to bring their claims into harmony with one another. These claims are always divergent and often seem incompatible. ... [The] three tyrannical masters are the external world, the super-ego and the id', (*New Introductory Lectures on Psychoanalysis*, p.110.)

The superego, like the id, is also largely unconscious. We develop it by internalising our parents' morals and standards during childhood. Having a harsh superego does not necessarily mean our parents were harsh or highly moralistic: our unconscious can turn their moral standards into something far harsher and more punitive than they were. If they were appropriately firm, for instance, we could have distorted this so that in our mind they were harsh. Or sometimes, when parents set too few rules and boundaries, their children may develop a harsh superego to compensate.

8: Paranoia

President George W. Bush, CNN.com/U.S, 6 November 2001 Posted: 10:13 p.m.

Klein, M. (1946), Notes on some schizoid mechanisms. In *Envy and Gratitude and Other Works 1946–1963*, Hogarth Press, 1975. Republished by Vintage, 1977.

Klein, M. (1957), Envy and gratitude. In *Envy and Gratitude and Other Works* as above.

10: Losing the Plot

Bion, W.R. (1961), *Experiences in Groups*, Karnac Books.

Basic assumptions: Bion contrasted a 'work group', where a team is connected to reality and focussed on their work, and 'basic assumption' states of mind which teams under stress can slip into unconsciously. He identified three basic assumptions:

'dependency', in which the unconscious assumption is that the team's real purpose is to depend on a leader, as seen in **Losing Agency**;

'fight/flight', in which the team seeks out a leader who will lead the fight or flight from their enemies. It's described in **The Looking Glass** (though unnamed);

'pairing', in which a team focuses on the future in which a pair – perhaps an existing leader and an expected recruit or a leader with an idea – will solve all their problems. This basic assumption is illustrated in **Losing the Plot**.

Two further basic assumptions were identified:

Oneness, by Pierre Turquet in 1974, in which group members are joined together in complete unity and all differences are seen as external; *Me-ness*, by Gordon Lawrence, Alastair Bain and Lawrence Gould in 1996. In this state of mind, the group is seen as dangerous, so the unspoken, unconscious contract is that members remain individuals, and not a group.

11: The Poison of Envy

Klein, M. (1957), *Envy and Gratitude* (see **Paranoia** above).

Klein thought envy stemmed from our destructive drive for death. It is mitigated by gratitude, but if our envy towards someone is too strong, gratitude towards them becomes impossible. Klein's work with young children showed that from early in life we feel grateful to those who care, support and protect us, and our gratitude builds and reinforces our love for them. Since gratitude and love go hand in hand, if envy dominates our personality overall, our capacity for love is affected.

12: Turning a Blind Eye

Chris Hanby, *New York Times*, 20 January 2020. Updated 15 June 2020.

Steiner, J. (1985), 'Turning a Blind Eye: The Cover-up for Oedipus', *International Review of Psychoanalysis*, 12: 161–172.

13: Repeating Patterns

Freud, S. (1914), Remembering, Repeating and Working-Through. In *The Standard Edition of the Complete Psychological Works of Sigmund Freud Volume XII* (1911–1913).

Freud, S. (1920), Beyond the Pleasure Principle, in *SE, Volume XVIII* (see **Life and Death** above).

Freud, S. (1926), 'Inhibitions, Symptoms and Anxiety', in *SE, Volume XX*.

15: Losing Agency

Bion, W.G. (1961), *Experiences in Groups*, London: Karnac Books (see **Losing the Plot** above).

16: Illusion

Winnicott, D. W. (1971), Transitional Objects and Transitional Phenomena. In *Playing and Reality.* First published by Tavistock Publications Ltd. Reprinted, Brunner-Routledge 2001.

At the beginning of life, the baby sees itself and its mother as one. The parent reinforces this illusion by responding immediately when the baby is hungry, so the baby has the illusion that he or she wanted something and created it. This omnipotence helps establish baby's psychological security. In time, as the baby can manage more, the parent gradually disillusions the baby by, for instance, responding less instantly to baby's demands. As a result, the baby starts to comprehend the difference between themselves and their parent or, as Winnicott put it, between 'me and not-me'. And, as they face the disillusionment in not having their every wish instantly fulfilled, the baby begins to adapt to reality. As Penny and Vanessa's story shows, we continue to use illusion as a defence and it's commonly behind wishful thinking.

17: Difference and Discrimination

Klein, M., see **The Looking Glass.**
Sundak, Marita, 'Everything you need to know about the movement against skin whitening', *Vogue India*, 10 September 2020. Skin-lightening products in India are

worth $450 to $535m annually, representing 50 per cent of the country's total skincare market.

Professor Gary Younge, 'We Can't Breathe: What connects the most brazen forms of state violence against black people and the struggles of BAME coronavirus patients is systemic racism', Newstatesman.com, 3 June 2020.

18: Changing Patterns

Barenboim, D. (2008), *Everything is Connected: The Power of Music*, London: Weidenfeld & Nicolson.

Barenboim, D. and Said, E. (2003), *Parallels and Paradoxes: Explorations in Music and Society*, Bloomsbury.

Barenboim, D. (2008), *On Life and Music*, Film transcript, Landseer Films, commissioned by Southbank Centre and Aksonas Holt, pp.20, 80, 88.

Barenboim, D. (2008), talk at the Royal Festival Hall as part of the Beethoven Sonata Cycle.

Braun, G. (2009), Wiederholung: Zwang oder Bereicherung? [Repetition: Compulsion or Accumulation?] In *Freie Assoziation, Volume 14, No. 2*, Germany, 2011.

Freud, S. (1920), Beyond the Pleasure Principle, in *SE, Volume XV111* (as above).

Dr Kadiatu Kanneh, at a musical tribute by the cellist Sheku Kanneh-Mason and his family to George Floyd following his murder on 25 May 2020. https://www.udiscovermusic.com/classical-news/kanneh-mason_family-george-floyd_tribute/

Kinderman, W. (2006), 'Beethoven's Piano Sonatas', in *Barenboim on Beethoven, The Complete Sonatas*, DVD set, EMI.

Kinderman quotes Maynard Solomon, Beethoven's biographer, who suggested that artistic masterpieces 'are instilled with a surplus of constantly renewable energy – an energy that provides a motive force for changes in the relations between human beings – because they contain projections of human dimensions and goals which have not yet been achieved', Kinderman, W, *Beethoven*, p.265 (Oxford University Press 2009).

West–Eastern Divan Orchestra, https://west-eastern-divan.org/divan-orchestra.

20: Speaking the Unspeakable

Bion, W. G. on nameless dread: see **Barriers and Barricades.**

Garland, C. (ed.), *Understanding Trauma. A Psychoanalytical Approach.* Second Enlarged Edition, Tavistock Clinic Series, First published in 1988, Gerald Duckworth & Co. Ltd. Reprinted 2022, Karnac Books.

Grossman, D. (2003), *Death As A Way of Life: From Oslo to the Geneva Agreement*, New York: Picador, p.7.

Jacoby, I. (2006), *My Darling Diary, Volume Two, The Girl in and out of Love. Oxford 1944–1950.* Cornwall: United Writers, p.392.

21: Being Ourselves

Winnicott, D.W. (1960), Ego Distortion in the True and False Self. In *The Maturational Processes and the Facilitating Environment: Studies in the Theory of Emotional Development.* First published 1965, Hogarth Press Ltd. Reprinted 1990, Karnac Books.

22: Kindness

Phillips A. and Taylor B. (2009), *On Kindness*, Penguin Books, pp.106, 107, 116.

23: Looking Back to Move Forwards

Didion, J. (2005), *The Year of Magical Thinking*, Fourth Estate.

Freud, S. (1917), Mourning and Melancholia, in *SE, Volume XIV* (1914–1916).

At the End

Faulkner, W. (1951), *Requiem for a Nun*, first published in Great Britain by Chatto & Windus, 1953. Published by Vintage, 1996, reissued 2015.

Acknowledgements

My deepest gratitude to my psychoanalyst who helped me in extraordinary ways. His talent, skill, compassion and care never wavered as we excavated, understood and changed my inner world and, as a result, my outer world. This book would not have been possible without you.

Mike Brearley began consulting to me when I ran a seminar series on leadership and psychoanalysis and stayed the (very long) course with me as I wrote the book. I have benefited enormously and thoroughly enjoyed the discussions we have had over the years. Mike's thinking and feedback are imprinted in the book, which wouldn't be what it is without him.

Wayne Milstead was my writing teacher, mentor and editor on earlier versions of the book. Working with him turned me into a writer. Wayne and Aaron run Circle of Misse, a lovely place of writing courses and retreats, which provided the perfect environment on several occasions.

Thank you to my family and friends whose encouragement helped me to keep going and means so much to me. I am particularly grateful to Birgit Kleeberg and Ann Simpson for listening to many chapters in many versions and thinking about the book with me for all these years.

Antonia Gillum Webb and Jed Elijah Staton played an

important part in the early stages of this journey. Thank you both. Thanks too, to the Conservatoire for Dance and Drama for hosting the original seminar series that sparked the idea of the book and to The Body Shop for hosting the next series.

I am indebted to Dame Ruth Silver and the Further Education Trust for Leadership (FETL) for boldly commissioning a project about psychoanalysis and systems thinking for leaders in the Further Education and Skills sector. The project was a highlight of my career. Many thanks to the participants for making it such an enjoyable, rich and rewarding experience.

Working with David Armstrong on the FETL project was key to its success and enjoyment. He encouraged me in my idea of taking psychoanalytic and systems thinking to a mainstream audience from the outset, is always supportive and always adds much to my thinking.

Matthew Hamilton, Nigel Wilcockson and Bella Lacey, thank you for your early encouragement.

Stephen Grosz's excellent book, *The Examined Life*, affirmed my idea of writing about psychoanalysis for a mainstream audience.

Huge thanks to Imogen Pelham, my lovely and terrific literary agent. From the moment Imogen got involved, writing no longer felt solitary. Her warmth, responsiveness and support, along with her clarity and spot-on feedback and advice have made an enormous difference to the book and to me. She set the book on its way and has been there for me throughout the journey.

I couldn't have hoped for a better editor than Holly Harley, who is a gem. Like Imogen, she completely got my book from the start. Her sensitive and astute editorial suggestions improved it immeasurably yet, like the fabulous book midwife that she is, she was always true to my vision of the book. Thank you so much, Holly.

I feel very lucky to have landed with Piatkus and the wider team at Little, Brown. With Holly's lead, they have steered my publishing journey with great expertise and enthusiasm. Special thanks to my lovely publicist Jess Gulliver, who secured some amazing opportunities and was so supportive; Sophie Harris who designed the brilliant cover; Jillian Stewart, editorial manager; Sarah Thomas, such a careful and patient editorial assistant, and Aimee Kitson, marketing.

Thank you also to those beyond Little, Brown who were an invaluable part of this process: Aruna Vasudevan, copyeditor; Jane Howard, proofreader and M Rules, the typesetters. And huge thanks to Tabitha Pelly, an incredible freelance publicist, who I was lucky enough to work with for this paperback edition and who made such a difference.

The camaraderie and support of the Debut 2022 authors has been an unexpected, added bonus and pleasure of publishing.

Thank you so much to all my students, supervisees, course and workshop participants.

Many thanks to those who kindly fact checked (and corrected) some chapters.

Finally, my heartfelt thanks to my clients. Working with you has been a privilege and taught me more than I can say.